Life...

Great advice, simply put

Life...

Great advice, simply put

Easy ways to get the most out of life

Edited by **Peggy Northrop,** Global Editor-in-Chief,
and the staff of READER'S DIGEST magazine

Published by The Reader's Digest Association, Inc.
London • New York • Sydney • Montreal

Life... Great advice, simply put
Published in 2012 in the United Kingdom by Vivat Direct Limited (t/a Reader's Digest),
157 Edgware Road, London W2 2HR

Life... Great advice, simply put is owned and under licence from The Reader's Digest Association,
Inc. All rights reserved.

Adapted from **Life... the Reader's Digest Version** published by The Reader's Digest Association,
Inc. in 2011.

We are committed both to the quality of our products and the service we provide our customers.
We value your comments, so please do contact us on **0871 351 1000** or visit our website at
www.readersdigest.co.uk

If you have any comments or suggestions about the content of our books, email us at
gbeditorial@readerdigest.co.uk

FOR VIVAT DIRECT

Editorial Director Julian Browne
Art Director Anne-Marie Bulat
Managing Editor Nina Hathway
Trade Books Editor Penny Craig
Picture Resource Manager Eleanor Ashfield
Prepress Technical Manager Dean Russell
Production Controller Jan Bucil
Product Production Manager Claudette Bramble

Book code 400-607

ISBN 978 1 78020 135 1

Printing and binding Arvato Iberia, Portugal

'The healthiest response to life is joy.'

– DEEPAK CHOPRA

'Take life with a grain of salt... a slice of lime
and a shot of tequila.'

– UNKNOWN

'Life is meant to be lived.'

– ELEANOR ROOSEVELT

Contents

DO BETTER 88

INTRODUCTION

Life seems to get more overwhelming every day – so much so that change is the new normal. Complexity is expected (along with 24/7 tech support), and everything happens at supersonic speed and comes in a dozen different flavours. No wonder so many people feel lost or just left behind by it all.

That's why the editors at *Reader's Digest* decided to step in and make this vast, sprawling adventure we call life a bit more manageable and lots more enjoyable. We think it's time to regain an element of control – to sit comfortably once again in the driver's seat and decide when to speed up, slow down, turn left, turn right – all the while remembering to enjoy the scenery.

At *Reader's Digest* we've been sifting through the wisdom of the world for nearly a century to publish a magazine so robust yet elegantly handy that it fits into a pocket. Now we've applied that same strategy to *Life... Great advice, simply put,* the handbook they never distributed in school. It's the heart-to-heart talk you should have had with your mother. It's the common sense advice you were supposed to gather along the way but didn't know where to look. It's the digested insight of seasoned men and women who've been there and done that and are now willing to share the road signs and directions to a life well lived.

On the pages that follow, you'll find succinct advice on some of the most essential facets of life, organised around ways you can **BE BETTER** and ways you can **DO BETTER.** You will discover clever workarounds, smart solutions to sticky problems and practical approaches to everyday challenges.

You will unearth nuggets of life-changing truths that run the gamut from health and wealth to loss and love, and from the sublime to the just plain smart.

When you're done, you'll know how to think big, get great seats, worry less, do more, find a mentor and get a good night's sleep. You'll be able to mix a perfect martini, talk your way out of a parking ticket and say what's on your mind. And all while wearing the perfectly ironed white shirt!

You may want to read this book straight through, or put it on a shelf and use it like a cookbook, reaching for a special recipe whenever the occasion calls for it. Either way, we invite you to scribble notes to yourself and capture memories and wisdom of your own in the margins. (Look for the write-in boxes scattered through the chapters – and think about how much fun it will be for you – and your children – to encounter your own thoughts about life in later years.)

We believe that a happy, successful life isn't hard to pull off. All that's needed are clear, practical, well-thought-out instructions and the ability to take a few minutes to pay attention to them. *Life...* is your GPS. It tells you where you are and lets you know whether to turn, reverse or keep going straight ahead. It's simple, reliable and ready for immediate use.

May it make your journey a little easier, brighter and more fun along the way.

PEGGY NORTHROP
GLOBAL EDITOR-IN-CHIEF

Be better...

Teach someone to fish and you feed her for a lifetime. Teach her how to unearth a long-buried dream to scuba dive among the manta rays and her soul may be sated for just as long. The intangible things we wish we had aren't always skills; they're often qualities, like self-awareness, kindness, gratitude, determination. How would our lives be different if we had what it takes to **BE BETTER** – think bigger, act nicer, seem smarter, feel calmer? If each day we made ourselves and those around us that much happier to be here? In this section, you'll learn everything from how to find yourself, to how to forgive, to how to leave the planet better than you found it. Scuba mask optional.

Think big

How do you reach a goal, change your life, realise a dream? If you delve into the backstories of successful people, a common theme emerges: they think big. Take former corporate executive Mary Lou Quinlan, who took time off in 1998 to ponder what she really wanted to do. She put up a folding screen in her home office and tacked index cards on which she'd written her goals at the top of each panel. What was she looking for? She wanted her own business, she wanted to be a paid public speaker, she wanted to write books, and she wanted to be on television. For the next few months, she brainstormed with friends, clipped news articles, showed up at conferences, and shook hands. In 1999, she launched Just Ask a Woman, a marketing company, and has since written several books, delivered hundreds of lectures and been a judge on a TV show. 'I didn't do everything from day one,' she says. 'But the picture was there 12 years ago.' Here's how to turn your own dreams into big-time success.

Be persistent

'People who are successful know themselves, and that means knowing what their talents are, knowing their capacity for work,' says Quinlan. Fear of failure? Big thinkers know nothing about it. Stubbornness? Big thinkers know a lot about that. 'You're going to stumble; you're going to run out of money; people are going to try to talk you out of what you want to do,' says Quinlan. 'And you have to be willing to push through.'

Tell the world
Write down your goals, then say them out loud to yourself and to anyone else who'll listen. 'That makes it harder to back out,' says Quinlan. Making it public also increases the chances that you'll find other people who can help you make your big idea a big reality.

Prepare to be uncomfortable
High achievers think they can do anything. No matter what task you put in front of them, the response is, 'How hard can this be?' They assume they can climb Everest when they've never even gone on a hike. 'I don't think I ever thought twice about failing,' says Quinlan. Nevertheless, she adds, 'you have to be humble enough to know what kind of help you need, to get where you want to go. When I joined a writers group, I had already run an ad agency, but here I was, sitting around a table with people who had successfully published books. It was like being in first grade again.'

Know when to listen
'When you have a big idea, 99 per cent of the people you encounter will tell you why it's a bad one,' says Victoria R. Brown, founder of Bigthink.com, a global ideas forum. Sometimes it *is* a bad idea. The trick, says Quinlan, is to know the difference between those who are jealous of your drive and those who wish you well and truly want to help by pointing out the pitfalls. 'Mostly, people are just throwing their own fears on you,' says Quinlan. Immunise yourself against naysayers by doing your homework. See who else has succeeded in your area of interest.

What did they learn along the way? Do you yearn to be an entrepreneur? Before you invest a lot of time or money, make sure that the product or service you have in mind isn't already on the market. Then, once you're sure your big idea is also a great one, roll up your sleeves and get to work.

BIG IDEAS - BIG RETURN These three big thinkers went from a 'eureka'! moment to changing the world.

▸▸ **Starting a revolution:** After seeing her friend gunned down by the security forces of former Egyptian president Hosni Mubarak, 26-year-old Asmaa Mahfouz posted a video of herself on Facebook imploring her countrymen to protest against the government. It went viral, and thousands came to Tahrir Square. Mahfouz's vlog was the spark that lit the Egyptian revolution.

▸▸ **Saving the planet:** The artificial trees created by geophysicist Klaus Lackner absorb carbon from emissions sources such as vehicles and residences. The Institution of Mechanical Engineers estimated that a forest of 100,000 such trees could mop up half the United Kingdom's carbon emissions, making the forest thousands of times more effective than its natural counterparts.

▸▸ **Feeding the hungry:** In 2009, US entrepreneur Navyn Salem got tired of news stories about childhood hunger and malnutrition around the world always ending the same way – with the problem getting worse instead of better. Believing the challenge could be met by applying business strategies, she established Edesia, a non-profit company, to mass-produce a nut paste that can stop malnutrition in young children. She hired 16 employees, many of them refugees, and within one year, she'd received a US$2 million federal grant to produce around 300,000kg of the food supplement, enough for more than 100,000 children.

Make a tough
decision

Too often, when faced with a fork in the road – whether relocating halfway across the country or having a child – we fret and dither so long that choice is no longer an option. Letting circumstances decide our fate is hardly the best way to get the most out of life's opportunities. Luckily, there's more to good decision-making than merely going with your gut. When you know how to do it, the hard choices seem almost clear-cut.

The mind-body connection

You can't make a good choice on a bad day. When you find yourself too anxious to analyse things, shift gears. Go for a run. Go to sleep. Resetting your body often opens your mind to a new perspective.

You first

Think about who you are. As Roy E. Disney, nephew to Walt and the man often credited with revitalising the family business, once said, 'When your values are dear to you, making decisions becomes easier.' Also a factor: how people close to you will be affected by the choice. Do not, however, use others as an excuse to head down the wrong path (for example, 'I have to save for the kids' university fees; therefore, I must accept this 80-hour-a-week job').

Accept the unknown

It's natural to want to figure out all the what-ifs before taking the plunge, but like calculating pi to 1,000 places in your head, it simply can't be done. The sooner you accept that there will always be some degree of risk involved in your choice, the more confidence you will have in making it.

Don't act impulsively, but also don't wait so long that you can't make the choice yourself.

Nothing is set in stone
Before you decide, give yourself permission to change your mind. Life is full of second chances. But don't reverse course just because you encounter one or two obstacles. Transition and change require time and effort. Make a serious commitment to your choice.

Let the rest go
You've made up your mind, so now stop dwelling on options you didn't choose. Believing in your decision is critical to achieving success.

GETTING IT RIGHT David McDermott, MD, a former surgeon who now teaches neurolinguistic programming, says you can make even the smallest choice easier if you follow the steps of a basic decision-making model:

1. **Define the situation and be clear about what you want.** Make sure you know exactly what is at stake and what you want to achieve. Define your goals in positive terms rather than in terms of what you don't want.

2. **Generate a list of alternatives.** In order to choose, you need to have options – even if there are only two.

3. **Gather information.** Weigh the pros and cons; bring your experience to bear; do research if necessary. Do not obsess.

4. **Make a selection.** Choose the most appealing alternative. You may be choosing rationally or intuitively – both are valid processes as long as you've followed the steps.

5. **Take action.** Don't just choose on paper; execute your plan.

Be better...

Get out of
a rut

'When you're finished changing,' Benjamin Franklin once said, 'you're finished'. But how do you know when you're running in place? Here's a hint: every day looks the same as the one before it and the one to follow, and you can move through the paces of your daily life with your eyes closed. That hairstyle – haven't you had it since secondary school? And isn't that jumper you bought a dead ringer for the five already in your wardrobe? It's time to shake it up. Find out what you've been missing.

Take stock of things

Doing the same thing the same way day in, day out can feel safe and familiar and comfortable – but follow the script long enough, and eventually the cocoon starts to feel more like a jail. Says marketing guru Seth Godin: 'We're human; that's what we do. We erect boundaries, and we get trapped.' Take a good, hard look at your life – your schedule, your activities, your relationships – and ask yourself whether anything new ever happens, whether there are ever any surprises, or if you feel like you're learning and growing personally and professionally. If the answer is no, you're in a rut.

Take it easy

You don't have to give yourself a whole life makeover to get unstuck, and you certainly don't have to do so all at once. Quitting your job, putting your house up for sale and dumping your significant other in the same week will certainly throw all your cards in the air, but it won't necessarily refresh your perspective. The changes you make can be minute – small but meaningful steps in a brand-new direction – but still end up packing a powerful, rut-busting punch.

Take a different route

Sometimes the best way to change gears is simply by varying your routine. Skip the motorway and follow the back roads to work. Go and see a film that's in a language you've never heard before. If you usually head to the gym each Wednesday for a madly energetic spin class, go for a long, thoughtful walk instead. Move everything out of your living room, and put it back in an entirely different arrangement – or swap half of it with stuff from elsewhere in your house. Pretend to be a tourist in your own town; go to restaurants, shops, or museums that aren't your usual haunts. The idea is to see the world through new eyes.

Take a leap

If little tweaks aren't moving you forward, maybe you need to try a new career, pull the plug on that stagnant relationship or relocate to another city. Sure, the shock may take your breath away at first, but that's the point. As Godin says, just 'deal with the pain, and then run forward. Fast.'

Of course, if your goal isn't to dye your hair a new shade of blond but rather to shave it off, move to Tibet and join a Zen monastery, you might want to talk about it first with people you know and trust and then map out a concrete plan. Think about

Be better...

how you might test-drive your experience. Taking a two-week leave from work to live in Barcelona or to do a volunteer stint on a kibbutz may be all you need to feel engaged in your life again. And if you're still feeling restless? Go ahead and take the swan dive from the 10-metre platform. After all, as novelist Ellen Glasgow once said, 'The only difference between a rut and a grave are the dimensions.'

Finding that spark

Christian Parsons works in a field (advertising) where ruts are a professional liability. On his blog ideadrunk.com, he lists 40 ways to jump-start anyone stalled in the same old, same old. Here are ten.

1. *Show up to work an hour earlier.*

2. *Talk to an 8-year-old.*

3. *Talk to an 80-year-old.*

4. *Build something with your hands.*

5. *Dance.*

6. *Call the smartest person you know and ask him or her to lunch.*

7. *Write a letter – with a pen.*

8. *Tour an art gallery.*

9. *Spend an afternoon at Toys 'R' Us. Buy LEGO.*

10. *Eat a punnet of blackberries.*

Have you ever taken a 'leap'?

Be a good
neighbour

'To have a good neighbour, be a good neighbour.' It's the golden rule of residential life. Things don't always play out like that, though, thanks to chain saws, drills, barking dogs and countless other public and private nuisances your own good example can't fix. Here are some of the best ways to avoid conflict.

Invite your neighbours to your parties

If you welcome those who live nearby to your outdoor parties, one of two things will happen: either they will come or they won't, but they will inevitably be prepared – and perhaps more forgiving – if one of your guests ends up skinny-dipping in their pool or if they are forced to listen to the thrum of Motown past their bedtime. You are not obliged to invite neighbours to your quiet indoor parties, although doing something nice for no reason is the definition of neighbourly.

Be friendly, but not overly so

Fences *do* make good neighbours. Real and virtual boundaries are healthy when it comes to your neighbourly relationships. Be pleasant, of course, and offer a cheery wave when you see your neighbour mowing the lawn. After all, a civil relationship just may blossom into a true friendship. Generally, though, the appropriate level of intimacy between neighbours allows for one neighbour to accept a package delivery for another, for example, but not to appear in the kitchen to deliver it without knocking first.

Be better...

Don't rush to judgment

If a neighbour does something that bothers you, don't be quick to assume it's intentional or out of ill will. Your neighbour may have no idea that his kid's daily garage-band rehearsals drive you crazy or that you can even hear them. A low-key heads-up may be all it takes to clear things up.

Don't rush to call the cops, either

And don't complain to the local council. That's practically shooting a flaming arrow from your garden to his. Before you involve a third party, try to resolve the issue immediately and directly with your neighbour. That's what a *good* neighbour would do.

IT COULD BE WORSE In 2008, US website tvsquad.com identified the 'nine least-wanted TV neighbours':

▶▶ Gladys Kravitz from *Bewitched*

▶▶ Cosmo Kramer from *Seinfeld*

▶▶ John Allen Hill from *Cheers*

▶▶ Glenn Quagmire from *The Family Guy*

▶▶ Steve Urkel from *Family Matters*

▶▶ Eddie Haskell from *Leave It to Beaver*

▶▶ Ned Flanders from *The Simpsons*

▶▶ Marie and Frank Barone from *Everybody Loves Raymond*

▶▶ Jerry Helper from *The Dick Van Dyke Show*

Be happy

Don't worry, be happy... Forget your troubles. Come on, get happy... We sing the songs, but we're often not really living the dream. Former lawyer Gretchen Rubin spent a year kicking the tyres of studies and theories about how to be happier. She chronicled her search in the book *The Happiness Project* and highly recommends that people do their own at-home version. 'Identify what brings you joy, satisfaction and engagement,' she says, 'and also what brings you guilt, anger and boredom. To boost your happiness, identify the concrete actions that will give you more of the former and less of the latter. Then comes the interesting part: keeping your resolutions.' Here are a few methods for upping your own happiness quotient.

Try something new

People who are always learning things and challenging themselves tend to be happier than people who get stuck in routines. No one says you have to go skydiving, but if you're a foodie, book a table at that just-opened Thai place. Love crafts? Take up knitting. The point is to branch out. The more you know, the more you'll find there is to know. And apparently, the more you're learning, the happier you'll be.

Take a nap

It may not be your idea of letting loose, but according to Rubin, fatigue is a major reason people are in a bad mood. Getting more sleep gives you more energy to do the things that make you happy, she says. And being sleep deprived can make you feel less like exercising, which she found is an extraordinarily important component for happiness.

Do what you like

Most of our days are built around what we *have* to do. So make sure the time you aren't working or studying or caring for others is spent on things you *like* to do. Read a novel, go to the movies or head to a museum or park. Did we mention exercise? Getting some fresh air and sunlight and revving up your heart rate with a brisk walk rarely fails to lift the spirit.

Channel your inner five-year-old

Ride your bike – to nowhere. Waste time on frivolous activities, laugh out loud, sing, dance, skip, play. Walk on the grass – preferably without shoes. Stop worrying about what happens next, and just enjoy the fun, the here and now. Seize the moment, and be a child again.

Give

Mother Teresa once said, 'Give until it hurts,' but you don't have to go that far. Donating time, money or things can make you feel happy and secure. And studies have determined that people who volunteer are healthier, have fewer aches and pains, and even live longer, says Rubin.

Join

There's happiness in numbers. We're social animals, and joining a group – book, athletic, gourmet, anything in which the members are connected by a common interest – helps to grow the social ties that add to our personal happiness. Think you're not a joiner? Put a bunch of people you like in the same room with snacks and just try not to smile.

Reclaim your space

The fewer messes you have to look at, the more peaceful and contented your mind will be. Take a few minutes to clear the decks or at least tidy them. Sort papers; respond to long-unanswered emails and voicemail messages. And then enjoy the space you've cleaned out both in your head and on your desk.

What makes you happy?

LOOK WHO'S HAPPY

▸▸ 80 per cent of Scandinavians are happy to go to work versus 50 per cent of Hong Kong's workforce, according to a survey conducted by Lumesse, a talent management firm.

▸▸ Carlisle is Britain's happiest city, according to a 2012 survey of more than 25,000 people by property website Rightmove.

▸▸ People working in the biotech field are happiest in their jobs, careerbliss.com reported.

▸▸ As a group, baby boomers are less happy than other generations. The boomer generation also reported feeling lonely, with those in their 50s feeling more isolated than those in their 70s, a report by Saga says.

▸▸ Children who identified themselves as spiritual – defined as having a strong sense of personal worth, a sense of value in their lives and deep interpersonal relationships – are 27 per cent more likely to be happy, according to a US study, which found that actual religious practice had no bearing on happiness.

▸▸ A 2012 Government study measuring well-being showed that mothers who stay at home are as content and satisfied with their lives as those who choose to go out to work.

▸▸ Couples who wed are more content than others, and those with children feel a greater sense of purpose, says the same report. And the young and old are both happier than the middle-aged who struggle with worries over jobs, mortgages and high costs of living.

▸▸ In the US, members of the clergy are 509 per cent happier than petrol pump attendants, reports the University of Chicago's National Opinion Research Centre.

Right a wrong

It turns out that Stacy in Marketing is *not* pregnant. (Oops.) It took you a month to return the lawn mower you borrowed from a neighbour. You bailed on your promise to help a friend move. Now you need to say you're sorry – and mean it.

An apology that's genuinely felt and properly delivered can be a powerful tool, whether the infraction is big or small. Of course, once we admit we blew it, the other person gets to tell us exactly how much we botched it. Worse, she may decide that forgiveness is out of the question. No wonder apologising is like taking a nasty swig of castor oil. Here's how to mean your *mea culpa* and make it go down a little easier.

Empathise

Understand the feelings of the injured party so you can frame an appropriate apology. 'Put yourself in her shoes,' counsels etiquette expert Lisa Gaché. 'This will help validate her feelings while also conveying your sincerity.'

Own it

Take full responsibility. The person whose feelings you stomped on does not want to hear phrases like 'Mistakes were made' or 'No one's perfect'. And please, no qualified apologies like 'If I've hurt you, I'm sorry', 'If I did anything wrong, I'm sorry',

'To the degree that you were offended...' Those 'apologies' will usually be tossed back at you like a cold drink in the face.

Make amends

You've owned up to your bad behaviour and asked for forgiveness, but your work is not done. You also have to repair as much of the damage as you can. You showed up 45 minutes late for a lunch date with a friend? Lunch – *with* dessert – is on you. You took credit for work not your own? Go to the boss and come clean. Linda Kenney, a mother of three, almost died 12 years ago when anaesthesia was improperly administered before her ankle surgery. She'd planned to sue until the anaesthesiologist sent her a letter expressing his grief and contrition. And then her doctor went even further: he started an organisation to help victims of medical error.

Correct your course

If you really want your apology to stick, assure the aggrieved person that it won't happen again. And then make sure it *doesn't*. If you patch things up only to make the same mistake over and over, you're showing that your words aren't sincere and you don't care enough to change your behaviour. Most people will accept an apology and give you a second chance. But they probably won't stick around to give you a third or fourth.

What was the most meaningful apology you've ever given or received?

Learn something new

People say it's never too late to learn something new, but like a lot of things people say, it ain't necessarily so. If you're in your fifties and want to start training to become a concert pianist, you'd better live to be a hundred. (Or, like Bill Murray in *Groundhog Day,* have one day to live over thousands of times.) Even if you're just out of uni, society finds a way of telling you that the time for learning is over. Nothing focuses the mind like the prospect of paying the rent! But if you have realistic expectations and remain diligent, you can master some new skills – whether writing a sonnet or riding a unicycle.

C'EST MAGNIFIQUE!

Be better...

Bake a cake

Susie Quick, author of *The Cake Club,* gets asked about making pies and baking cakes by newbies of all ages. 'My number one piece of advice would be to buy a baking book from an expert, with simple recipes to follow,' she says. 'You need one with lots of techniques explained and a glossary of baking terms.'

The idea isn't to learn to make everything in the book, but to become familiar with how baking works in order to develop your instincts. 'It's best to be a master of a few perfect desserts and breads than an amateur of many,' says Quick. Nevertheless, you should look at every cake recipe you can get your hands on to hunt for tips and tricks. And order a slice every time you see it on the menu – you need to know what the competition is up to.

Speak a new language

While it's been proved that young minds absorb new languages with greater ease than grown-ups, that's no excuse not to try to communicate with more of the world. After all, thinking in another language keeps the brain agile.

According to Simon Ager of the popular language-learning website Omniglot (omniglot.com), total immersion is the ideal way to learn. But if you hope to speak Russian and can't afford a trip to Moscow, head to an area or town or borough whose residents hail from there. Or find a native speaker of whatever language you want to learn in your town and ask to speak only in her language. She'll be flattered.

Finding time is the biggest hindrance, according to Ager, whose advice is '*Carpe momentum*'. 'Even if you only study for five to ten minutes at a time, it all adds up in the end.' Try listening to Chinese radio, reading Arabic newspapers or watching a foreign language film with subtitles and see how far you get.

Play an instrument

As any professional will tell you, the secret to learning how to play a musical instrument is quite simple really: 'Practice,

practice, practice.' Even if you'll never play in a space bigger than your living room, there is no sense in picking up the guitar, sax, violin or glockenspiel unless you can devote at least a half hour a day to the pursuit, and ideally two hours or more. In fact, in his best-selling book *Outliers: The Story of Success*, author Malcolm Gladwell claims that the key to mastering *anything* comes down to practising it for approximately 10,000 hours.

Once you've committed yourself to 'woodshedding' – as the pros call practice in private – find someone in your area who can give you lessons or at least assess your musical ability. Online resources and software help you, but nothing beats an actual teacher when you're getting started. If you don't feel comfortable with your first teacher, try another. Even in a small town, there will be several musicians trying to make a few pennies on the side. Above all, enjoy yourself. Don't see your lessons as a way to impress anyone or be put off if you don't progress as quickly as you would like. Music should be fun.

Count your blessings

We all have 'to do' lists. But we should probably spend more time on our 'to thank' lists. Health, family, friends and special talents are often taken for granted unless they're threatened. Reminding ourselves of the good in our lives also helps take the sting out of the bad.

See it

Gather images and words connected to the happiness in your life: family photos of a day at the beach, postcards of places where you had fun. Make a 'blessings board' that hangs near where you work or relax. Your daily outlook will be brightened by these reminders.

Write it

Use a gratitude journal to record the day-to-day events that make you happy. Take time before bed to flip through it and reflect on what has been going right. Maybe you received a compliment at work, found a £20 note in your jacket pocket or spotted wildlife on your morning walk. Reading through past entries can reset your attitude on dull or dreary days.

> 'We can only be said to be alive in those moments when our hearts are conscious of our treasures.'
>
> – Thornton Wilder, American author

Imagine it

If today isn't going the way you had hoped it would, take a few minutes to picture how you'd like your life to be. That's what Olympic athletes do before competing – they visualise their perfect performance, then try to achieve it. What do you want to do that you haven't? That perfect future may not be as far off as you thought.

Lose it

If you find yourself singing too many bars of 'Woe is me', commit to striking complaints from your vocabulary for a month (OK, maybe three weeks). To stop yourself from whining about petty disturbances, count to 10 or count your blessings – whichever number is higher.

Read someone's
body language

If you've ever watched a film without the sound and managed to follow what's happening, you're reading body language – the way the characters communicate with their hands, face, even posture. Studies confirm we continuously (and unconsciously) size up the intentions of a stranger by their physical demeanour. But when it comes to people we're more familiar with, we often fall short.

'It's more difficult to read friends and family members because we invest people with a halo or horns,' says Carol Kinsey Goman, PhD, author of *The Silent Language of Leaders*. 'If we like them, we see only the good; if we don't like them, every message they send is suspicious.' Here are a few basic principles to help separate the sincere from the sleazy.

If someone's lying

No single gesture gives a liar away. Some members of the species can even look you straight in the eye and go undetected. However, says Dr Goman, 'When you know someone well enough to know what his baseline behaviour is, you can also know what his stress signals look like.' Lots of blinking, a flushed or perspiring face, or a fake smile (real smiles crinkle the eyes) – these may indicate that someone isn't levelling with you.

If someone disagrees

What if your mate or colleague is saying one thing and you sense it means something else? 'There's probably some mismatch between gestures and facial expressions and the words you are hearing,' says Dr Goman. If she genuinely likes or agrees with what you're saying, her body will show it. Signs of engagement include leaning forward and connecting with the eyes. If she's just glancing at you or even slightly turns her body away from you, this indicates she's not into what you're proposing, no matter what she says. That's when you know you should revisit the topic.

If you're doing the talking

Make sure you're perceived as being honest by smiling, maintaining eye contact and facing someone head-on every time you hold a conversation. This signals that you're interested in what's being said and usually improves both the conversation *and* the relationship.

If you're dealing with a child

Young children are easy to read because they haven't learned the art of dissembling yet. A toddler with chocolate on his face will say he did not eat that biscuit. 'A child just beginning to experiment with lying might even put her hand over her mouth, meaning, "I can't believe I said that!"' says Dr Goman. 'Babies will fake cry just to get attention, a trick they start using from the time they are a few months old.'

As children get older, adult behaviours begin to take shape. At that age, there's a fine line between self-awareness and self-consciousness so tread carefully when pointing out what their body language signals. But don't leave them in the dark. 'Parents [can/should] help their children understand how we can tell when they are angry or that they love us [without even saying a word],' says Dr Goman.

What's the dead-giveaway gesture someone close to you uses?

Be more satisfied
at work

Ask most people what would make them happier on the job and they'll probably say more money, more flexibility and a boss who doesn't breathe fire and sprout horns on a regular basis. All worthy goals. But it's the little things – those hundreds of interactions you have with colleagues from 9 to 5 – that have the biggest impact on how you view your work life. Here are some quick and easy ways to improve your outlook.

Take the high road

Like a YouTube video of a waterskiing hamster, negativity among colleagues spreads fast. The difference is that when grumbling and gossip go viral, it's not just harmless fun. Yes, it's tempting to complain about your boss or to pass on that rumour about the new guy's drinking problem, but resist the urge. If you can't, you'll eventually be known as someone who can't keep her mouth shut. All it takes to make clear you're not playing is to say, 'I'm not comfortable hearing that' or even 'You don't say!' Then smile and move on.

Talk to your boss

The number one reason people quit their jobs? According to a Gallup poll of more than 1 million people, the answer is a bad boss. 'People leave managers, not companies,' conclude the pollsters. The truth is, your boss may be difficult, inaccessible or just not very helpful. But if you learn to communicate well with her, you're more likely to come to mind first when new opportunities like a promotion arise. That means knowing when to bring up concerns, doing so clearly and honestly, and listening carefully to her response – even if you disagree.

Share credit

The best way to get the credit you deserve is to share it with others, according to Stephen Viscusi, author of *Bulletproof Your Job: 4 Simple Strategies to Ride Out the Rough Times and Come Out on Top at Work*. 'You look good for whatever you've done, *and* you look even better for being confident enough to share it with others,' he writes. The flip side of sharing credit is sharing blame. And while you should spread the credit around whenever you can, you should share the blame very rarely. Take responsibility for your own stuff, and never single out another person in public. If pressed by your boss to explain who did what when things went wrong, do it very carefully and avoid finding a fall guy.

Stay cool

When you're aggravated or angry, ask yourself if whatever upset you is important, says anger management consultant Virginia Williams. Is what you're thinking and feeling appropriate to the objective facts of the situation? Can you modify the circumstances? Is it worth taking action? If so, do it after you've calmed down and mapped out a thoughtful strategy. And don't let yourself dwell on the offence. Find a way to distract yourself – plan your dream vacation, read a favourite poem – when you get steamed on the job.

Go with it

When a work colleague shares feedback about your work, accept it as information, not criticism. Although it may be your first instinct, don't react defensively. If you think the critique is off base, privately ask a third party for assessment. But don't dwell on it. Hear it, consider it, decide what to do with it – and move on.

ONE MORE REASON TO BE NICE AT THE OFFICE If your feelings towards your fellow workers are only slightly less hostile than Tim Canterbury's towards Gareth Keenan in *The Office,* you might want to try a little harder – or at least stop stealing their staplers and encasing them in jelly. A recent study published in the journal *Health Psychology* has found that people whose work environments offered the most social support – whether chatting around the coffee urn or working on a group project – had a lower overall incidence of death over a 20-year period than those whose workplaces were more stressful. And those benefits persisted even after adjusting for factors like blood pressure, alcohol consumption, gender and education level. Another study indicates that workers who receive support in the form of constructive feedback, encouragement and compassion from their workmates have lower blood pressure than those who don't. So think about joining the office football team. It might be good for you in more ways than one.

Be better...

Make a good
first impression

You don't get a second chance to make a first impression – in fact, you barely have any time at all the first time around. A series of studies at US university Princeton found that all it takes is a tenth of a second to form a gut feeling about a stranger, and that longer exposures don't significantly alter such snap judgments. So if you want a good shot at wowing someone, make sure you've paid attention to every last detail that gets noticed at first glance.

In a job interview

Dress in clothes that flatter and fit you properly and that won't distract your interviewer – or you. 'Interview attire needs to hit the right balance between friendliness and formality. A well-fitted suit is confidence in instant form,' advises *Men's Health* magazine. 'If you have a pale complexion, navy will suit you far better than grey, and shows more imagination than black.' Women should avoid dangly jewellery, low-necked tops and bare legs. Don't forget to trim your nails and floss your teeth, and when you meet with your interviewer, avoid shaking her hand across a large desk – leaning and stretching can be awkward for both of you. And use his or her name twice in the first 15 seconds, suggest Allan and Barbara Pease in *The Definitive Book of Body Language*. That helps you remember it, and it makes the conversation seem more personal. Do your homework about the person interviewing you and the company he works for so you come off as well informed about both.

At a party

Take the lead. Approach a stranger, and be the first to extend your hand and introduce yourself. Start the conversation on common ground by asking how he knows the host. This will immediately establish rapport, what Nicholas Boothman, author of *How to Make People Like You in 90 Seconds or Less,* calls 'a comfort zone where two people can mentally connect, each bringing something to the interaction.' If he's with his wife, ask how they met, which is sure to lead to an anecdote they'll love to tell. Let them tell it. Offer to refresh their drinks when they've finished their story, and say something flattering before going off to mingle: 'Bob has always said what a great couple you two are. I'm glad I finally got a chance to meet you both and see what he means!'

At a parent/teacher evening

You're not just there to shoot the breeze; you have an agenda – to establish a relationship with the teacher, a connection that will be an asset to your child throughout the school year. So rather than diving right in to talk about your child (and seeming like an overeager stage parent), try some small talk first. 'For instance, say how nice the classroom looks,' says Angela Engel, a child education advocate and author. Follow up with a question that will elicit specific information: 'Where did you get those leaf stencils?' Avoid questions that require a yes-or-no answer, such as those that begin 'Are you?' 'Do you?' or 'Have you?' Rather than building a rapport, those words 'will have you playing tennis on your own against a brick wall,' says Boothman. When it comes to your child let the teacher do the talking first. Give her the opportunity to say her piece without interruption. Tilt and nod your head as she speaks, to indicate 'I hear you, and I agree.'

With someone you already know you don't like

If you're meeting a person whose reputation precedes him, give him the benefit of the doubt. You may be pleasantly surprised. Keep things cordial and light, and always exhibit good manners. It's to your advantage that he respects you, even if you never become best buddies.

WHEN MEETING SOMEONE FOR THE FIRST TIME These rules apply to all sorts of situations:

▶▶ **Observe body language.** Whether sitting or standing, keep your back straight – avoid slouching. Turn your body towards the other person. This pose signals that you're friendly and receptive. Don't cross your arms or legs (this suggests the opposite). Take your cues from the other person's behaviour – her tone of voice, the pace and content of her speech and her gestures.

▶▶ **Pay attention.** Listen for nuances in what others say. 'When people ask a question,' says communications expert Susanne Gaddis, PhD, 'they are subtly steering the conversation to what they want to talk about.'

▶▶ **Keep it light.** Don't whine. No one wants to hear you complain about the traffic jam on your way to meet your child's best friend's mum, whom you absolutely can't stand. Be positive and upbeat.

▶▶ **Show respect.** Be on time (and get there early if it's a job interview). Turn off your mobile phone, and don't look at your watch. Show genuine interest. Ask questions that show you're listening, but don't dominate the conversation. Smile, shake hands when you part, and say, 'Nice meeting you!' as if you mean it.

Has anyone ever wowed you the first time you met?

Lose yourself

Life can be chaotic and complicated. And breaking free of the madness can sometimes seem like madness itself. (Turn off, drop out – me?) But when you're going at full tilt, are burnt out or undernourished, you don't need to find time – you need to lose all track of it. Here's how.

Disconnect
Turn off your mobile, your computer, the TV – even the lights. Completely disengage from the buzz, chatter and information that bear down on you every day. Don't answer the door; don't answer email; don't answer the phone. Do it for a day – or do it for an hour if that's all you've got.

Put one foot in front of the other
Walking is one of the best ways to bring yourself back into sync. Choose a part of town you don't know, and just wander. Stroll up and down the main roads and every little side street. Duck into bookstores and secondhand shops. Stop by the local school's football game. Relish being a visitor in someone else's world.

Just drive
This one is simple: get in the car and take off. Pick a direction you don't normally go in and set out on the open road. Don't look at maps; don't make plans; don't turn on the GPS. Just drive until you're hungry or need to stretch your legs. Pull over when you see somewhere interesting. Get out, breathe deeply and take in your surroundings. Then get back in your car and keep driving.

Disappear
This takes a little planning if you want to keep your job and your house. Tell your boss, your mate or your family that you're taking a little 'me time'. Choose a destination that's unlike the

places you usually visit. Stay in a place that isn't your usual style. You ordinarily like room service? This time, check into a B&B. Eat in small restaurants. Buy a book to read when you get there. Try a little oath of silence. Travel light. Return renewed.

LOSE YOUR MIND Getting lost isn't about a destination but a state of mind. It's about being somewhere that evokes, inspires and allows free or creative thought that you're just not getting in your daily life. You don't have to scale Machu Picchu. Maybe you need go no further than the pond in the local park, the cheese stand at a farmer's market or the shelves of your local library. Now go on, get out of here!

Look 10 years
younger

The game's up. Bar staff no longer ask to see proof of your age, and you hear 'madam' or 'sir' a few times a week. You live in fear that you may be just one day away from being offered the senior citizens' discount at the cinema. But ageing doesn't have to be this way. And looking significantly younger – whether you're a man or a woman – doesn't require surgery. There's more to it, however, than applying a good moisturiser and some sunblock (although both are crucial). Here, from all natural to man-made, are some of the best ways to shave a decade off your looks.

Run the clock back

We all know exercise is 'good' for us, but did you know it could reduce your biological age and make you look younger? Thirty minutes of moderate cardio five times a week will regenerate your cells, eliminate toxins from your body and create a youthful glow. And while eating healthily is always important, this is no time for extreme dieting. The French tell us that at a certain age, women in particular must choose between the bottom and the face. So don't despair over a couple of extra pounds; a little fullness in the face plumps out the lines.

Sleep on it

If you're tired, there's a good chance you're going to look older: during the deep sleep you *should* be getting, cells grow and repair the damage caused by stress and ultraviolet rays – it's literally beauty sleep, so don't short change yourself. And try to lie on your back – many dermatologists believe that sleeping face down on a pillow or primarily on one side, will cause wrinkles in your skin over time.

Be better...

Just do it

Studies have proven that in addition to boosting self-esteem and confidence, frequent sex with a regular partner increases the production of human growth hormone, which is known to improve muscle tone.

Feed your skin

Antioxidant-rich foods (high in beta-carotene and vitamins A, C and E) slow the effects of ageing and correct skin damage. What to put in your anti-ageing shopping cart? Sweet potatoes, pecans, berries, broccoli, cabbage, cauliflower, Brussels sprouts, tomatoes, garlic, spinach and carrots.

Soften those lines

While there's no genie in a bottle when it comes to zapping wrinkles, you can minimise them by applying a lotion with alpha hydroxy acid each morning. It makes skin look smoother by sloughing off old skin cells and stimulating the growth of new ones. At night, use a product containing retinoids – these vitamin A derivatives work to neutralise the unstable oxygen molecules that break down skin cells and lead to wrinkles.

Handle with care

Your hands will give you away faster than your birth certificate. Moisturise them religiously, constantly, aggressively. As with face creams, ones with retinoids and alpha hydroxy acid will make skin look less wrinkled. Use a lotion fortified with 2 per cent hydroquinone – a bleaching agent – to treat any age spots. Women should keep in mind that dark nail polish and long nails can draw attention to veiny or sunspotted hands.

Whiten up

A bright, white smile will take years off your face, whether you opt for a professional whitening job or the very effective whitening strips and gels available from your local chemist.

Cut, colour and condition your hair

Get rid of the grey, decrees Charla Krupp, author of the best-selling book *How Not to Look Old*. For men, the salt-and-pepper look is fine, but they should get any colouring done professionally. Women should think about going a shade lighter and getting face-framing highlights, as well as getting a short cut, which provides a softer frame around the face than longer hair does. Women who love long locks need to spend the time and money to keep them highly conditioned and trimmed; left on its own, hair gets drier and more brittle, a telltale sign of where someone really is on the actuarial charts.

GOING PRO Still unhappy with the way your face is ageing despite a drawer full of over-the-counter treatments? If you're despairing over wrinkles or age spots and determined to do something about it, head to a clinic performing non-surgical cosmetic procedures, where your best bets are these procedures, according to Dr Minas Constantinides, director of facial plastic and reconstructive surgery at NYU Medical Centre in the US:

▸▸ **Botulinum toxin injections** Known by the brand names Botox and Dysport, these injected chemicals work by paralysing specific facial muscles, thus preventing the contractions that lead to wrinkles. **Best for:** crow's-feet and frown lines that are visible when squinting or frowning. **Lasts:** three to four months.

▸▸ **Fillers** If you've heard of Restylane or Juvéderm, then you're familiar with the injections of hyaluronic acid dermatologists use to plump up facial areas that are lined or have lost volume over the years. **Best for:** deeper wrinkles, thin lips, hollow cheeks and sagging jowls. **Lasts:** between six and nine months.

▸▸ **Chemical peels** By applying a solution containing acid to the face, a doctor can remove the outer, damaged layer of skin or at least speed up the process of shedding it. The extent of the damage being treated determines the strength of the solution and the acid used. Within a few days of treatment, the skin cells begin to peel off. **Best for:** uneven pigment, wrinkles (fine to deep), sun damage. **Lasts:** one month to several years, depending on the treatment.

▸▸ **Laser and light therapy** Lasers and intense pulsed light (IPL) treatments, which work beneath the surface of the skin, are another weapon in your derm's arsenal when it comes to turning back the clock. You'll need four to six sessions of IPL to see results. **Best for:** fine lines and wrinkles, uneven pigment, sun damage. **Lasts:** up to a year or even longer.

Be aware this is an unregulated industry, so make sure you have any procedure done by a qualified and experienced practitioner, says Dr Constantinides. For those carrying out injectable treatments, consult the Treatments You Can Trust register (www.treatmentsyoucantrust. org.uk), backed by the Department of Health. And while cosmetic procedures like these aren't usually available on the NHS, don't be tempted to skimp. This is one area where looking for a bargain can cost you.

What's on your age-masking to-do list?

Write
a letter

BTW, IMHO EMI isn't 4NE thing and everything. KWIM? What we're trying to say here is that in our humble opinion, email does have its place. So do texting and twittering. But there are certain occasions when 140 characters or an alphabet soup of abbreviations and textspeak are not adequate or appropriate. Sometimes what's required is an actual letter. BYKT, right?

Covering letter with CV

One size fits all may be true of ponchos. It's not true for covering letters. You must customise each one to fit the job you're after, says Kathy Klein, vice president of Global Employment Solutions. Begin by saying what you think the job is, 'then explain how your experience makes you a good fit,' she says. Also use the letter to explain CV red flags – for instance, gaps in your employment history, short-term positions or a lot of relocations. 'You want to reassure a prospective employer that you're in town for good,' says Klein. Be diligent in the details. Even if you're a whizz at spelling and grammar, ask a trusted friend to proofread your work. You're so familiar with the contents of the letter that you're apt to read right over mistakes. Don't end with the presumptuous 'I'll call you in two weeks.' 'That makes me think, 'Oh, so you're taking my time twice – first by sending your CV, then by calling me,'' says Klein. Instead, go with a courteous 'Thanks in advance for reviewing my credentials. I look forward to hearing from you.'

Letter to the editor

Stick to the guidelines on a publication's website, letters column or editorial page. If the suggested limit is 300 words, don't give them *War and Peace*. Get to the point quickly, back it up with facts and sign off. Stay on topic – if you're writing to protest about high council taxes, don't rant about school kids who throw rubbish in your front garden – and avoid profanities and emoticons.

❝This is not a letter but my arms around you for a brief moment.❞
– Katherine Mansfield, author

Thank-you note

There is no substitute for this one. You do not get out of it if you didn't ask for the gift, if you don't like the gift or if you said, 'Hey, thanks,' when it was handed to you. Get out a pen (preferably blue or black ink) and a piece of stationery – a plain white or off-white card will do. The note doesn't have to be long (three sentences is just fine), but it must mention the gift, your delight in it (try to be specific – 'I wore it last night and got so many compliments!'), and your appreciation for the sender's thoughtfulness. And what you write must *sound* like you. Saying that the cakestand is 'absolutely stunning' when words like that have never crossed your lips will come across as insincere. Write the note as soon as possible. At the very least, this lets the sender know the present arrived at its destination.

Condolence note

The note should be hand-written rather than typed. What you say and how much you say depends on how close you were to the deceased or to the family. But, as with a thank-you letter, a few well-chosen handwritten sentences will generally suffice. Phrases like 'I'm so sorry,' 'She was such a wonderful person,' 'He was the model of the man I hope to become,' and 'I'll miss her, too' will help you connect with the recipient. You needn't restrict yourself to expressions of sympathy. If you have a favourite anecdote about the deceased or some particular memory you cherish, by all means include it. But avoid comments like 'She's in a better place,' 'It was God's will,' and 'At least he isn't suffering any more.' Leave that for those closest to the deceased to say – when they're ready.

Be the perfect
party guest

Y ou know when that guest everyone is waiting for has arrived. There's a shift in the energy of the room. People around him become more animated, convinced that *this* is the place to be. There is suddenly more laughter, and space starts to open on the floor as the focus switches to the new centre of attention. He's happy to be there, and having him there makes other people happy, too. People want either to *be* him or be *with* him. You might not be the straw that stirs the drink, but you can be much more than just one of the cubes by being the Perfect Guest.

Play the game

A famous actor once revealed why he always seemed so happy on TV talk shows. 'I prepare myself – I do an acting exercise,' he said. 'I tell myself I'm playing a character who's enjoying himself.' So it is with a party. The Perfect Guest is in character; he *knows* he's where he's supposed to be. He's not wishing he could be home watching the game or playing FarmVille. He works the room like a practised politician, lighting on this one and that one – an air kiss here, a man hug there – not sinking into conversation with any one person for too long but making everyone feel special for a moment.

Be the barman
Who needs a barman when the Perfect Guest shows up? He's happy to pour the wine and crack open the beers, and he knows how to mix a mean martini and a minty mojito. He takes a load off the host by making sure everyone's drink is fresh. He's got a drink in his own hand, but he's not drinking much. He doesn't have to – he's already enjoying himself.

Make the connections
The Perfect Guest knows how to make people comfortable. She can listen to your cares, then make you laugh and forget about them. She works hard (without showing it) to find what two strangers have in common. 'Wasn't your daughter thinking of going to university in Nottingham? Ted and Alice here have a second home in Nottingham!' And once the connection is made, she slips away to connect some other wayward dots.

Never let the party drag
A good party is like a good movie. You shouldn't be thinking about it too much when it's happening, but instead, on the way home, you'll want to rehash everything: 'Did you talk to that guy from Ethiopia?' 'I'm so glad that people were dancing!' or 'Wasn't that cake amazing?' The Perfect Guest never lets things drag. If someone starts playing music no one wants to hear or goes on and on about some point that doesn't matter to others, he gently redirects the course and guides the party through the rocky shoals.

Wrap it up
When the host starts making signs that it's time to leave, the Perfect Guest knows how to help wind things down by turning

down the music, turning up the lights, helping with coats. Then he secures his position as treasured friend and all-time great party asset by helping the host or hostess clean up. Nothing says 'The party's over' like someone hauling out black bin liners. Politely, of course.

WHEN KIDS ARE INCLUDED A kid at an adult party is always a wild card. Everyone has seen that miserable child, the one who could blow at any minute. When the Perfect Guest spies a tired, sad or overwrought little girl in the corner, he engages her on her level. If she has her nose stuck in a book, he talks knowledgeably about what she's reading. But if it's a miserable toddler demanding attention, he knows it's time to pull a coin out of the kid's ear or, better yet, make a balloon animal.

Here's how:

BALLOON DOG

1. Blow up a modelling balloon, also known as a 260 or pencil (5cm by 152cm), halfway and tie it off at the end.

2. Starting with the balloon's knotted end, make three sets of three twists every 10cm, resulting in three short sections and one long section.

3. Twist the second and third sections together to form a circle; these are the dog's ears.

Be better...

4. Make three additional sections with three twists 10cm apart.

5. Twist the second and third of these new sections so they hang on the underside of the balloon's body. These are the dog's front legs.

6. Make three more sets of three twists 10cm apart.

7. Twist the second and third of these new sections together to form the dog's back legs.

8. The final section is the dog's tail.

9. Reconfigure the first four sections (the dog's neck, ears, and snout) so they point up.

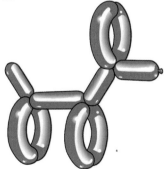

10. Present to the child and watch her smile.

Forgive

A friend, work colleague or family member has betrayed your confidence, taken credit for something you did, broken a promise, failed to deliver big-time. Maybe the person who did you wrong has expressed remorse and a desire to make amends. You, however, stay stubbornly in the 'Forgive? Forget it!' camp. This isn't fortitude, it's foolishness. Clinging to anger and resentment only keeps you from getting over what happened and getting on with your life. Or, as one anonymous wag put it, 'Holding a grudge is like drinking poison and hoping the other guy will die.' In other words, forgiveness is ultimately for *you*.

Forgiving isn't forgetting

'It takes enormous strength of character to forgive someone,' says *Reader's Digest* columnist Jeanne Marie Laskas. 'But forgiving doesn't mean pretending it didn't happen. That would be just setting yourself up to be walked all over. When someone steps on your foot, you say, "Ouch". You have to acknowledge the hurt to give the other person a chance to say sorry, so then you can say, "I forgive you".' That's when you can let the hurt go, along with all the rage and resentment. If you can think back on the situation and remember what you learned from it but don't feel the anger or hurt the way you did when it happened, you have successfully forgiven.

Come clean

You may be tempted to hide your anger or hurt, especially if it means avoiding a confrontation with the person who did you wrong. But as Laskas reiterates: 'The perpetrator may not even be aware that you were hurt. You're angry, and the other person doesn't even know it.' (This is a staple plot device on the more tedious reality TV shows.) Be direct, and confront the person with *your* hurt, not *his* shortcomings. 'Talk to the person the way you would prefer to be spoken to,' Laskas advises. Discuss how the incident made you feel – no yelling or name calling. Otherwise, you're only going to put the other person on the defensive. Say your piece, stop being a victim and stop dwelling on the incident, the perpetrator and your revenge fantasies.

Be prepared

Even after laying out the particulars of your pain, you may not get the *mea culpa* you're looking for. If saying 'I'm sorry' isn't what the perpetrator has in mind, 'forgiveness becomes a much bigger challenge,' admits Laskas. 'If you request an apology and it's not forthcoming, wipe the person off your list. It's a toxic relationship. Maybe the apology will come later and you can re-evaluate.'

> 'The weak can never forgive. Forgiveness is an attribute of the strong.'
> – Mahatma Gandhi

GET OVER IT – FOR YOUR HEALTH According to a report by the medical research group Mayo Clinic, hanging on to a grudge appears to affect the cardiovascular and nervous system. In one study, people who focused on their resentment had elevated heart rates and blood pressure as well as increased muscle tension. When asked to imagine letting bygones be bygones, the participants said they felt more positive and relaxed. Down dropped their systolic and diastolic numbers. Down went their heart rates. Down went their stress. Get it?

Remember **names**

You vividly recall the pattern of the floor tiles in your school's assembly hall, so why can't you manage to summon up the name of that friend of a friend as he approaches you in the cereal aisle? Is it Mike? Mark? Matt? You're drawing a blank because the two pieces of the puzzle actually reside in two different places: the image of Matt's face is in your brain's right hemisphere, but his name is in the left. Getting the twain to meet is simple if you rely on this technique from memory expert Benjamin Levy. (The acronym, FACE, is one even fuzzy-headed types can remember.)

BILL!

Focus

When you're meeting someone new, concentrate your full attention on him. Don't race ahead in your mind to come up with something to say. Instead, look the person in the eye, shake hands and listen carefully to his whole name as it's said. Don't release your grip until you're sure you've got it.

Ask

Speak the name back to the person in the form of a question. 'Hi, I'm Katherine. I'm sorry, did you say Don or Dom?' Or 'Robert, is it? Nice to meet you. I'm Katherine.' The brain responds more actively when a question is answered, so by repeating the name this way, you're increasing your chances of remembering it. To up the odds even more, try working in another question if possible: 'Are you Stephen with a 'ph' or a 'v'?' 'Ty... Is that short for Tyler?'

Comment

Next, tell yourself something about the name to ensure that it sticks. If your new acquaintance goes by Bill, make quick mental associations with famous people named Bill, relatives named Bill, or any other kind of bill. *Oh, his name is Bill. Like the movie,* Kill Bill, *my uncle Bill and my restaurant bill.* You might even try a visual trick and imagine your uncle giving *Kill Bill* director Quentin Tarantino the bill. Then, if appropriate, say something about the name, such as 'My favourite uncle's name is Bill.' Creating mental connections and supporting them with a statement said aloud further cements the name in your memory.

Employ

After repeating the name and then commenting on it, use it once or twice more in conversation. Do this either by addressing the person directly or referring to him while speaking to someone else ('Hey, Jim! Bill and I were just talking about that new Brad Pitt movie!'). When the conversation ends, use the person's name again: 'Bill, it was so nice to meet you.' Be careful not to overuse the name, though, since that can come off as awkward or insincere, says Levy.

A LITTLE HELP FROM OUR WIRELESS FRIENDS If you're an iPhone owner who is hopeless at remembering names, you might want to download NameCatcher, which Kelly Nowlin developed to combat what she calls 'hey, buddy–itis'. For less than the cost of a cup of coffee, this popular app allows you to enter names into your phone by category ('church', 'medical', 'salesperson'), then add additional search terms, such as physical attributes and other descriptors and even a photo. And it will sync to your contacts list. (That neighbour you see watering her garden every week, who wears bifocals around her neck and drives a red Honda? Now you can jog your memory using any of those prompts.) Nowlin, who frequents her local park, used the application to remember the name of someone whose pup had been injured and says the man seemed genuinely touched when she mentioned it. 'I sincerely do care,' she says, speaking for all foggy-brained types. 'I just might need a tool to help me remember here and there.'

What clever name games do you rely upon?

Be better...

Worry **less**

Worry can be so stressful, so wearying, so time-consuming. And to what purpose? Lots of the things we fret about don't come to pass. As Mark Twain once put it, 'My life has been an endless series of misfortunes, most of which never happened.' And even when bad stuff arrives with our name and address on the postage label, we're generally strong enough to deal with it, says Judy Christie, the author of *Hurry Less, Worry Less*.

Identify why your stomach is in knots
Identify what's keeping you up at night. Sometimes the simple act of writing down those anxieties – money, the jerk at work, the fight you just had with your spouse or children – can help you get a handle on things. Are there steps you can take to improve matters? If so, write them down, too, and then make a plan to act. If not, acknowledge that your worry is doing nothing but sapping your energy.

Lose the small stuff
Minor annoyances and pressures can provide fuel for bigger worries, so eliminate them. Allow a few extra minutes to get where you're going. Don't timetable appointment after appointment. Leave open spots in your schedule to take care of the logistics of daily life. The more room you give yourself to breathe, the easier it is to breathe without worrying.

Avoid rehearsing for tragedy
You can choose to look at a situation in a negative or positive way, says Christie. For example, instead of needlessly worrying about losing your job, focus on the joys in the work you do and imagine yourself happily and steadily employed.

Call a moratorium on worrying

Choose a chunk of time during the day when you're not allowed to worry – and when you're not allowed to worry about worrying. If you begin to fret, acknowledge the thought, turn the page on the thought and do something to change your focus.

Sleep on it

We often worry *because* we're tired, not the other way around. Don't try to make big decisions when you're worn out. Think of Scarlett O'Hara and tell yourself you'll worry about it tomorrow – after you're better rested.

Embrace change

The devil we haven't met – that's the way lots of us view change. As creatures of habit, we seek – and find – comfort in consistency and predictability. Switching jobs, schools or careers or just going from art deco to Danish modern may well turn out to be the greatest thing that has ever happened to us (or our living room), but it does involve endings and loss, and it also means directing our feet to that very scary address known as the unknown. But according to family psychologist Jennifer Hartstein, it's actually the anticipation of change that roils us more than the change itself. 'Once you've engaged in the new situation and realise it can be managed effectively,' she says, 'the anxiety and fear subside.'

Feel free to fret

Instead of judging yourself or trying to dismiss negative thoughts about change, remember that everything you're feeling is perfectly natural and understandable.

Move forward

When the ground is shifting around your feet, think about what you can do to lessen that unpleasant rocking motion. Say you're moving to a new city. Map out the step-by-steps that will get you there: bids from removal companies, friends to help you pack, online research about your new area. Identifying concrete, manageable steps and taking action can immediately make you feel more in control and also help you visualise the positives that lie ahead.

Find a cheerleader

When you find yourself clinging to 'the way things are' and avoiding changes that could represent fresh opportunities, turn to the people who believe in you and can help you feel confident and positive about the challenges you face.

Change the way you feel about change

Steve Frisch a clinical psychologist, says those most adept at adapting to the sight of new business cards or the moving truck at the front door are people who can reframe a situation. They find the upside to upheaval – like the chance for career growth, to start over, to make new friends. It's the businessperson saying, 'This job will give me a chance to increase my client base, but I'll still have my old clients.' It's the father-of-the-bride saying, 'I'm not losing a daughter; I'm gaining the son I never had.' Soon, says Dr Frisch, 'you will find yourself excited by what's ahead.'

Get your 15 minutes
of fame

The best kind of fame is usually a by-product of something else – inspiration, ambition, vision, drive. The other faces of fame – notoriety and infamy – aren't the ones we want to see when we look in the mirror. Here are a few ideas on how to succeed at the fame game using qualities that would elude the cast of *Made in Chelsea* on their best day.

Be better...

Develop a cult following

Be imaginative. When Thea Colman quit her job in estate agency to become a full-time mum, she couldn't turn off her entrepreneurial brain, even when she was enjoying her two favourite recreational pastimes – knitting and creating exotic cocktails. So three years ago she merged her two loves to create BabyCocktails, the hippest (and maybe only) knitting/mixology blog. Every month, Colman sells hundreds of her original patterns named for the cocktail recipes she provides. She has a worldwide fan club, has begun designing for yarn companies, teaches, and has become a local expert/celebrity/guru. And she still has time for a drink at the end of the day.

> ⟨Fame usually comes to those who are thinking about something else.⟩
>
> – Oliver Wendell Holmes

Become a hero

Do good. For Magnus MacFarlane-Barrow, it began about 20 years ago with the desire to do just one good deed. Seeing the suffering of children in Bosnian refugee camps, he and his brother took a week off from their jobs as salmon farmers in Scotland and delivered food, medicine, clothes and blankets to the camps. But when he returned home, he found his neighbours had donated truckloads more. MacFarlane-Barrow ended up making 22 trips. Shortly afterwards, he quit his job, sold his home and devoted himself to helping people in need, setting up the charity Scottish International Relief and later Mary's Meals, which feeds more than 500,000 children around the world every day.

Get your name in lights

Do what you love. Just because you never fulfilled your dream of becoming a big star doesn't mean you can't get some attention as a performer. If you've always wanted to tread the boards, find a community theatre group and get an audition. Most will require you to do a cold reading (reading off a script you've never seen before) or maybe a monologue. While you may not make it to the West End, you may just have the chance to get on stage and perform your heart out – and you'll have loads of fun along the way. If acting's not your bag, how about singing in a community choir?

Get more done

God created the world in six days, and then He took a day off. Well, good for the Almighty, but that's a luxury most of us don't have. There's just so much to do – and so many supposedly time- and labour-saving devices to complicate the process. We can't necessarily change our to-do list, but according to time-management expert Julie Morgenstern, we *can* do something about the sometimes cockeyed way we try to get it all done.

Make a plan
Don't just jump into the fray of your day; in fact, try to avoid the fray entirely. Morgenstern suggests that you sit down for five to ten minutes before the start of the working day (better yet, the night before) to plan what needs to be done and when. Draft a to-do list and assign times to various tasks throughout the day to keep yourself moving forwards.

Beat the clock

Set an oven or computer timer for 10, 15 or 30 minutes and challenge yourself to get as much done on a given task as possible. A deadline is a great motivator and a mighty aid in avoiding the mother of all distractions: the internet.

Stay focused

Turn off the phone and shut down email when dealing with tasks that require focus. When someone comes to you with a matter that can wait, *let* it wait. 'Don't be afraid to say, 'I'll have to get back to you later,' counsels Morgenstern.

Become a taskmaster

Don't avoid delegating around the house because 'it's easier to do it myself.' That attitude is both martyrlike and exhausting. Assign age- and time-appropriate tasks to everyone in the family, and you'll marvel at how much gets done. Outside the home, organise car pools or volunteer activities so you can trade off with others.

Break it up

Instead of writing 'clean the house' on your to-do list, break down the task into bite-size jobs. Wash the dishes. Do three loads of laundry. Vacuum the living room and bedrooms. You'll make faster progress and feel as if you've accomplished more.

Plan for unpleasant surprises

Is your doctor or airline running behind? Always carry around a book, a small organisational or planning project, a list of phone calls to make, letters to write (or read) or a knitting project. You'll have something to work on while you're waiting.

Be flexible

If something in the day's schedule doesn't work out, don't fret and don't miss a beat. Just move on to the next task. And don't be a slave to your to-do list. You don't work for your list; your list works for you. If someone invites you out for ice cream on a beautiful afternoon, *go*, says Morgenstern. Rest assured, the list will be there when you get back.

TO-DON'TS Overscheduling is a surefire way to undermine how much you can get done in a day – and make you feel as if you're underachieving, even if you're running around at a pace that would make an Olympic sprinter envious. On days when there's too much to do, review your list and remove anything that isn't essential. Perhaps the supermarket shop doesn't have to be done today. There's no blue ribbon awarded for taking on too much, so practise saying no from time to time. It gets easier with a little practice and will soon become an important time- and life-management tool.

Name three things you could delegate to others.

Go green (really)

These days, it's hard to fire up your laptop without seeing something about carbon footprints or canvas shopping bags. But does it really matter if your newspaper winds up with the coffee grounds rather than in the recycle bin? Can one person really affect the fate of the planet without moving to a teepee and sewing his own clothes? Think of it this way: if each of us turned the thermostat down two degrees in winter and up two degrees in summer, we'd prevent 900kg of carbon dioxide per person from entering the atmosphere each year – that's the equivalent of driving 7,725 fewer kilometres. And there are plenty of other ways to go green without going nuts. Read on.

Your house

A lot of it you've heard before. Be sure your home is well insulated and the windows well caulked, run the washers (clothes and dish) only when full, and turn the lights out when you leave a room. Since many appliances have a standby mode that siphons energy even when they're not turned on, unplug things like phone chargers, laptops, stereos and small appliances when you're not using them. (To make it easier, have multiple electronic devices plugged into one surge protector so you can power them all down with the flick of a switch.)

Wash your clothes in cold water, dry them on the line when the weather's nice and keep the lint filter clean when it's not. Read on a laptop, which uses 80 per cent less energy than a desktop. Want to get really radical? Ditch the microwave. Not only does it require lots of energy to run, but storing the frozen foods you cook in them – both in your freezer and in the huge supermarket ones – does, too, as does shipping them to you from the plant where they're made.

Your car

With petrol prices through the roof, you may be considering a hybrid or an electric vehicle to save money as well as the Earth. But if the car you have is still in good condition and gets 10 km per litre or more, you're better off hanging on to it, even though that hybrid might get an enviable 17km per litre; more than 25 per cent of the car's carbon emission is created during manufacture. If you keep your old car, be sure to get it tuned regularly, inflate and align the tyres properly, and remove non-essentials that may be weighing down the boot. (Hauling an extra 45 kilos can reduce fuel economy by 2 per cent.) Try to use the alternative modes of transport – you know, car pools, buses, bicycles, your feet. Planning to travel by air? Book a direct flight.

Your groceries

As you're scouring the aisles and checking things off your shopping list, follow these green guidelines:

▸▸ *Buy local, in-season produce. The alternative requires more energy to refrigerate and more fuel to ship. Plus, it tastes better.*

▸▸ *Avoid products with unnecessary packaging; bigger is better (and less wasteful) if you'll use all of it.*

▸▸ *Skip the paper napkins. Use fabric instead.*

▸▸ *Other things to keep out of the trolley: bottled water (filter your own instead) and incandescent lightbulbs, if you can still find them (they use up to 80 per cent more energy than energy-saving ones, which last up to 15 times longer).*

Oh, and you did remember to bring the canvas shopping bag, right?

TREE TIME If all that recycling, unplugging and running to catch the bus isn't for you, you can make just as much of a difference to the environment by planting a tree. Make that a bunch. Every one offsets about a ton of carbon emissions during the life of the tree. The Woodland Trust, who aims to create the biggest continuous native woodland in England, will plant one for you. Go to woodlandtrust.org.uk to donate or find out about different schemes to help you plant your own.

What things are you doing to help the Earth?

Be a good
parent

We read the books, the magazines and the blogs. We compare notes, swap tips and tell harrowing tales from the trenches. It's a wonder anyone has a second child. But in the end, being a good parent boils down to the questions we ask ourselves for 20 years and the answers we manage to come up with.

Don't try to make a happy baby happier
This is one of the best pieces of parenting advice we've heard, and it applies not only to sleeping babies (leave his blanket alone; don't adjust her head position) but to older children as well. If your kid is fine, let him be. You know those parents who chase after their happily playing tyke with a jumper or an apple, or their contented teenager with an idea about another class she could take? The term is 'helicopter parent'. Let the happy, healthy babies, toddlers and teenagers *be*.

Be consistent
Kids need routine from the very beginning. Not rigid or overscheduled, but general routine – rules about bedtime and television that stay the same. Adults in charge – that's what makes kids feels safe. Without consistency and limits to count on, the big wide world can be a scary place.

Listen
Kids of all ages get upset. It's how you respond that makes the difference. The tragic event may not seem earth-shattering to you, but if you've been listening, you will understand how it fits into the landscape of their world and why it matters. Don't dismiss it as trivial or (as tempting as it may be) laugh

it off. Instead, try to express real empathy. Either you will have something helpful to say or the hug you give will say it for you.

Set a good example

Children listen and watch – sometimes precisely when you wish they wouldn't. It's from you they learn to be polite, to volunteer, to keep their word and to read rather than watch reality TV. They get their values from you, every day in every way.

'We are always too busy for our children; we never give them the time or interest they deserve. We lavish gifts upon them; but the most precious gift, our personal association, which means so much to them, we give grudgingly.'

– Mark Twain

Spend time

'There's no such thing as quality time. There's just time,' actor-dad Timothy Daly told an interviewer, bemoaning his empty nest. 'I miss driving them. I miss coaching soccer,' he said. Then he excused himself to go and visit his daughter at college.

Let them be who they are

Some kids come out of the womb hardwired and fully hatched; they are who they are from day one. Others need to experiment and try out different versions of themselves along the way. At some point, either scenario may drive you out of your mind. Remember, you are there not to make them into who *you* want them to be but to help them become the best possible version of themselves.

Love them – out loud

Always. Unconditionally. Every day.

Appear
more intelligent

You *could* wear specs with plain glass lenses; celebrities do it all the time when they want to look serious. But we think it's better to hold your own in smart company by making an honest effort. (Note: by this we do *not* mean acting as if you're brainier than everybody else in the room. That's just off-putting – and stupid.)

Know your news

It is never OK to say 'What revolution?' if there's been one somewhere in the world within the past week. No one is suggesting you read every page of every paper of record every day. Instead, scan the news summaries and headlines on the front pages of the broadsheets for the top stories the smart people are paying attention to. Or check the breaking-news stories from the BBC, Sky, Yahoo! or mobile service providers on your smartphone or computer. These are updated constantly, and you can be on top of the news before you finish sipping the foam on your cappuccino. Supplement the headlines with news from whatever medium works best for you.

Talk the talk

Nothing will shave 30 points off your perceived IQ more quickly than bad grammar. It's the way certain people separate the wheat from the chaff. A few of the groaners to avoid:

- ‣ *less/few (You have less milk but fewer cups.)*

- ‣ *bad vs. badly (A person who feels badly has something wrong with his/her nerve endings; a sick person feels bad.)*

- ‣ *pronoun problems ('Between her and I' should be*

*'between her and me,' 'She and I went to the cinema,' not
'me and her.')*

▸▸ *the word 'hotel' is
pronounced with an H.
Trying to make a word
sound fancy does nothing
but blow your cover.*

❝ Knowing a great deal is not
the same as being smart;
intelligence is not information
alone, but also judgment, the
manner in which information
is collected and used. **❞**

– Carl Sagan, American astronomer,
writer and scientist

Keep it together

Organise your files, lists, paper
clips – all of it. A person who is
disorganised is often perceived
as being... well, a scatterbrain.
Once you've decluttered, go out
of your way to prepare for events; do a little homework
before you head into that meeting/job interview/dinner party.
People are flattered when they discover you know things
about them (not stalkerish things, of course). And when the
people you're talking to are flattered, they look good and you
look smart.

Spell-check

Seriously. This is one of the world's greatest inventions – maybe
better than the wheel. Use it religiously to correct your typing
mistakes.

Listen and ask

You're at a dinner party with your spouse and her colleagues.
She's a neuroscientist. You're a pastry chef. Don't pretend to
know the latest news about the amygdala. Just listen and ask
questions. It's OK not to know. And it's very smart to ask an
intelligent question.

Be comfortable **alone**

For some people, solitude fits as comfortably as a second skin. For others, it's like wearing a hair shirt. But being alone is not the same as being lonely (which can be achieved in a roomful of people). Loner or not, you'll be surprised by what cultivating your solitary side can do for your creativity, inner peace and even your relationships. In fact, learning to embrace and explore solitude might just lead you to the holy grail of contemporary life – balance.

Cut the static
Ever notice how the busier and more frenetic our lives are, the more appointments and meetings we pack in and the more buzzing, beeping, ringing, have-to-take-this gadgetry we tote along with us? Do you really need 852 of your closest 'friends' with you *all the time*? The opportunities for contact are endless; the ones for disconnecting aren't. Unplug and recharge.

Shed your skin
Let every role you play in your life fall away, like so many stifling layers of winter clothing. Spend time being neither mother nor wife, friend, employee, boss or daughter. Leave behind your identity as 'the funny one', 'the dependable one', or 'the one who needs to please everyone all the time'. What you are left with is... you. When is the last time you were alone in a room with just you? If you don't remember, chances are you have a lot of catching up to do. Enjoy it.

Lose the guilt
Overachievers take note: we don't have to be 'accomplishing' something or talking to someone every second of every day. Being alone is not 'down' time, and it's certainly not 'wasted' time. More often than not, it's the magic time when genius can happen.

Make a date with yourself

Not a born loner? Practise. Schedule a regular time to enjoy your own company. A date *with* you and *for* you. Go to a museum alone or grab lunch at an outdoor café. You will feel increasingly at home with solitude, and you'll realise your time is just that – yours.

ALONE AND LOVING IT If you love being alone, you have company. Famous introverts include baseball legend Joe DiMaggio, scientists Isaac Newton and Albert Einstein, literary recluse J. D. Salinger and billionaire Howard Hughes. And although she has become forever linked to the line 'I want to be alone', from the film *Grand Hotel,* actress Greta Garbo claimed later, 'I never said, "I want to be alone". I said, "I want to be let alone". There is all the difference.'

Recover from a gaffe

You're standing at your friend's birthday brunch sipping a drink, when suddenly, horribly, it dawns on you: your gift to the guest of honour that she is now opening in front of the entire room still contains the note from your mother-in-law wishing you a merry Christmas. There's a reason the word mortified, from the Latin *mortifer*, 'producing death', is used to describe the intense shame and humiliation you're now feeling as you look for the nearest trapdoor. But since one of those – along with rocks to crawl under – usually isn't nearby in such circumstances, your best recourse is to respond with tact, grace and humour. Here's how to deal with it when you've stuck your foot in a sticky situation.

Assess the damage

Things may not be as bad as you think. There are gaffes, and there are Gaffes. Did you drop a forkful of cauliflower under the table at a dinner party? Get someone's name wrong? Forget the winking emoticon when you emailed your coworker about sucking up to the CEO? In the case of such a minor stumble, deal with it discreetly – there's no need to draw huge attention to the matter. If you can't reach the cauliflower, leave it. If you've mistakenly called someone you've just met 'Jake', simply say, 'I'm sorry, Jack. I'm terrible when it comes to names.' As for the email that may not have come across quite right, offer a brief apology, making sure not to labour the point. 'Hey, Ed. I think my joke may have fallen a little flat. I didn't mean to imply anything by it.'

Take a breath

If your goof is more serious – you've insulted your boss or deeply wounded your mother-in-law's feelings – your first instinct may be to panic. But before you rush into the gaffe-fixing breach, gather your thoughts. Blaming someone else, tossing off a bad joke or making excuses are worse than no response at all. A better strategy involves careful consideration and perhaps even consultation with someone close to the situation. If you think about the consequences your actions have caused and how best to smooth things over, your odds of forgiveness will improve.

Admit the error

Take responsibility for the goof and apologise. Jacqueline Whitmore, etiquette expert and author of *Business Class: Etiquette Essentials for Success at Work*, says, 'It's not the mistakes but the way in which you handle them that will make or break your reputation. Owning up may be unpleasant, even distasteful, but it's the right thing to do.'

Defuse with humour

If you've made a public gaffe, you're often not the only one feeling uncomfortable, and sometimes a well-placed, self-deprecating joke can put everyone at ease. But don't push it: if the recipient of the insult isn't ready to laugh things off, skip the stand-up routine for now.

GUARANTEED GAFFES No doubt you've seen – or done – more than one of these big-time blunders. Avoid them and you won't have to engage in spin control later.

▸▸ Never comment on a woman's pregnancy unless you know for certain she's pregnant.

▸▸ Never assume two people are a couple (or aren't) based on their race, gender, age or earning power.

▸▸ Never address someone you don't know by his/her first name in business correspondence.

▸▸ Never post anything you wouldn't want your boss (or your mother) to read on your Facebook or Twitter accounts.

▸▸ Always check the recipient line of your email before you hit Send.

Cope with a **crisis**

It happens to us all, so we might as well learn to handle it well. If you lose your job, end a long-term relationship or lose everything to a natural disaster, your impulse may be to retreat to your bed and assume the foetal position. But if you're busy wringing your hands, how will you roll up your sleeves and start anew? Here's how to cope.

Feel free to freak out – but not forever

Let's say you've just been fired. Having an anxiety attack – pounding heart, tight chest, dry mouth – is to be expected. But you can't make rational decisions while in panic mode. 'Get present,' says psychotherapist Rhoda Pregerson. 'Feel your feet on the ground. Feel your back against the chair. Take note of the colour of the sky. Take note of your breathing,' she advises. Life coach John Dulworth encourages clients to push through the hysteria by repeating the words 'I'm here, and it's OK.' 'Accepting something doesn't mean you don't want to change it,' he says. 'But until you accept the problem or the situation, you can't begin to fix it.'

Remember that you're not alone

Ask for help from calm, logical friends or professionals. 'Remind yourself that this is normal stuff,' suggests Pregerson, 'and that in some form or another, many people you know have gone through a crisis and come out the other side.'

Check your vital signs

You can't vanquish a crisis on an empty stomach. You need to eat, drink, sleep and exercise. If you need to set a timer to remind yourself to do those things, do it.

Reframe the situation

Don't think of the crisis as something that happened *to* you (translation: you're a victim) but rather something that happened *for* you (translation: oh, this may eventually make things better). The job loss or the end of a relationship could be just the push you needed to do something you've always wanted to do – for example, start your own business or go back to university. A character in the *I Ching*, the Chinese book of divination, translates a crisis as 'a dangerous opportunity'. The key word, says Pregerson, is 'opportunity'.

Console someone

Children are easy: a hug, some whispered words of reassurance and a trip to the playground generally do the job. Comforting an adult can be tricky. Being available, sensitive and generous – these are key.

Let them cry

'As soap is to the body, tears are to the soul,' says grief-and-loss counsellor Jane Bissler, PhD. Crying can be cleansing and cathartic and may be just what your friend or family member needs to do at the moment. It may make you feel uncomfortable to watch, but sorry, this isn't about you. Deal with it – and go and find a big box of tissues.

Let the hurt hurt

Minimising the pain may simply make things more difficult for your grieving friend. Acknowledge the situation by saying something such as 'I know it's scary to lose your job' or 'A breakup is a horrible thing to go through.'

Follow the leader

We all want to feel useful, but sometimes being useful is not what a friend wants. She may simply want someone who can listen without passing judgment or offering advice. It can help to ask, 'I have some ideas about that. Would you like to hear them?' If you get a negative reaction, shift back into listening mode.

Know that little things mean a lot

A short email message, a bunch of flowers, or a coffee cake – these small gestures might be just what someone needs to feel better about things.

Lend a hand

Often, after an event like a death in the family, people need basic logistical help picking up family at the airport, making phone calls and food shopping. Step up to the plate with specific ways you can be of service. Be aware that your friend will likely need you even more in the days and weeks after the initial rush of support from friends and neighbours. Pay attention and step into the void if necessary – again with concrete offers to help. Bring over dinner. Babysit. Take her for a drive. Help weed her garden. Be there.

Be better...

Find **yourself**

Big birthdays invariably bring bad jokes about reading glasses and Zimmer frames, but they also prompt people to take stock of who and where they are in life. Ditto such seismic changes as divorce, the death of a loved one or a health scare. But there's no reason to wait for a milestone to have an 'aha' moment. Periodically taking a step back from your daily routine and engaging in some self-reflection can help you make sense of your place in the world: is who you've become who you want to be? To discover (or maybe just reboot) your true self – no matter where you are in your journey – try these techniques.

Take a good, hard look at yourself

And realise you might not like what you see. It can be discouraging to realise you aren't where you want to be in life, but don't use that excuse to stay stuck where you are. The same with the notion that your problems are everyone else's fault, from your mum (who didn't let you take ballet lessons) to your boss (who speed-dials you from bed at night). Take ownership for the person you are, commit yourself to making some possibly scary changes and be prepared to wing it when it comes to mapping out the new you. Says Loren Slocum, author of *Life Tuneups: Your Personal Plan to Find Balance, Discover Your Passion, and Step into Greatness*, 'There are no rules for what success looks like.'

Make time for yourself

One reason you may feel you're losing touch with yourself is that you're too busy taking care of the needs of everyone else in your life. Keep a diary of the way you spend your time for a week; account for everything. When you look at how your days are divvied up, you might realise how little is left for you. The solution? Delegate, outsource and give stuff up if you have to.

Then follow through with what life coach John Assaraf, author of *The Secret*, calls the 'art of GOYA – getting up off your a** and doing it!'

Schedule time on your calendar to reacquaint yourself with your passions. Go back to interests and activities you've neglected, whether that's painting watercolours or participating in a book group. And take an hour a week just to think about your personal goals and to strategise how you will meet them. Slocum actually sets her phone alarm to remind herself to keep pushing toward goals big and small. (Her daily 9 A.M. text message to herself: 'Breathe'.) 'Write something short – no longer than a tweet,' she says. 'People say they can't focus on their goals because the phone is always going off. Why not use the phone to actually help you meet them instead? Use technology to your advantage.'

Don't be afraid to make big changes

As a young professional working in law Gretchen Rubin seemed to be in exactly the right place. She believed she had her dream job – until, that is, she had an epiphany one rainy afternoon on, of all places, a city bus. Amazing as her life was, it wasn't the one she wanted. 'One reason I left law was that I [felt] I was... on a tangent, off-centre,' she writes on her blog, happiness-project. com. 'I asked myself, "What do I want from life, anyway?" and I thought, "I want to be happy" – but I never spent any time thinking about happiness.' Once she realised her real dream was to be a writer, her path became clear. Today she's an author of five books, including the best-selling *The Happiness Project*, an account of the year she spent test-driving studies and theories about how to be happier, and a regular contributor to *Good Housekeeping*. Her advice to finding the real you? 'Take small, concrete steps in your daily life.' (To read more of her advice, see 'Be happy,' page 22.) And keep checking in with yourself each week to make sure you're heading in the right direction.

'The biggest reason people don't achieve their goals is that they don't stop and take inventory enough,' says Loren Slocum.

Find support

Life coach, author and motivational speaker Tony Robbins said, 'Who you surround yourself with is who you become.' Find a mentor who is willing to counsel you as you start to switch things up in your life. If you don't have a friend to fill that role, seek out a professional. But before you spend money on a life coach, try first reading the autobiography of someone you admire or going on YouTube and listening to a motivational speaker you've always been curious about, suggests Slocum. It may be all the boost you need. And no matter where you find your inspiration, be open to ideas, but listen to your own instincts first and foremost.

Serve others

And not the ones who've become used to you picking up their dirty socks. We mean pitching in and helping those truly in need. Spend a couple of afternoons a week talking with elderly people at an assisted-living residence, helping out in a charity shop or handing out sandwiches at a soup kitchen. Offer to help an elderly neighbour with their shopping or just talk to them. Something as simple as performing five random acts of kindness a week can improve your mood and your sense of well-being. And when you feel better about yourself, you're more apt to tackle new challenges on the road to self-fulfilment.

What are your life goals?

Make friends

In an era of tweets and pokes, a 'friend' is anyone who asks you to confirm her as one on Facebook and then 'likes' your link to *The X Factor*. But after moving, switching jobs or just sending the kids off to university, you may suddenly find yourself with a daily support network that consists of the guy that serves you in Pret and the postman – and yearning for a few more meaningful connections. Here's how to brush up on skills you may not have used since your first week in college.

Put yourself out there

Instead of getting a takeaway and watching *Downton Abbey* DVDs alone after work, go where like-minded people are. Take a class, attend a concert, join an organisation related to your interests or profession. While you're at it, hook up with your school's old girls' organisation and buy a gym membership. It's easier to bond with people you have something in common with.

Follow up

When you meet someone you seem to get along with, ask to exchange contact information so you can get together again. Then (and this is the crucial part) get in touch within 48 hours, says networking guru Keith Ferrazzi, author of *Never Eat Lunch Alone*. If you don't circle back soon after your first meeting, you will have missed your best chance to deepen the connection – any later attempt may come off as halfhearted, insincere or, worst of all, desperate.

Say yes

If a new acquaintance asks you to do something with her, take her up on it, even if you don't think you have much interest in the sealife centre at 9 A.M. When you're further along in your friendship, you can be pickier about how you pass the time with her, and in the meantime, you may find you actually enjoy opera, bird-watching or Yogilates. Accepting invitations from someone new also increases the chances that you'll meet more people you click with.

Share relationships – but not confidences

Be generous with your social contacts, offering to connect people within your circle who you think would get along. You'll find the favour returned. As your just-forged friendships begin to blossom, be available and be loyal. Lend an ear when someone wants to confide in you, then keep it to yourself and don't gossip. While introductions on LinkedIn are nice, trust is the most valuable thing you can offer a new friend.

GO TO THE DOGS Dogs make great companions, not to mention great crutches for the socially awkward. Hit the street with your schnauzer, and canine-loving strangers will stop to pat him on the head and chat with you, too – no need to grope awkwardly for a topic of conversation when there's Pedigree Chum versus raw, organic to debate. If you've ever thought of visiting your local animal shelter, there's never a better time than when you're feeling the need for a few friends, whether four-legged or two-.

Have difficult
conversations

The truth can be harsh. But sometimes it has to be told, especially when the person on the receiving end is someone you care about. The good news: honesty comes in all shapes and sizes, and you can customise it for many of life's stickiest situations. 'You need to find language that gets your message across without destroying the other person,' says psychotherapist Sharyn Wolf. 'If you have to tell somebody something that is going to hurt them, it will hurt. But there are still better and worse ways to convey the information.'

With someone with bad breath
Bad breath after a garlicky lunch is like spinach in the teeth – she'll be glad you tipped her off. Offer her a mint or a piece of chewing gum and say, 'This will help you evade the garlic police.' If it's chronic, invite her out for a drink or coffee. Then get straight to the point: 'I hope you won't be offended, but sometimes your breath can be a little strong.' She may be upset initially, but one day she will probably thank you. If you're not close enough to the person to be that direct, offer her that mint or gum regularly, while complaining about your own breath. Eventually, she'll become conscious of her own problem.

With your soon-to-be ex
Wolf wrote five relationship books and then went through her own divorce – she knows whereof she speaks. If you're done with all the soul-searching and discussion and ready to declare your intentions, 'make it simple and clean,' says Wolf. 'If you really want out, there can be no hinting. You can't say, "I don't think this can work." You have to say, "I'm sorry, but this relationship is

over." Then follow up with "But I will do everything I can to keep things civil between us." ' Being clear and decisive benefits both of you, no matter how difficult the conversation might be.

With someone who's just too much
You know the type – she's too loud, talks too much, is too demanding. But you love her anyway. If she asks for advice or complains about trouble she's having and her character traits are the cause, try saying something like 'Sally, you have a big personality/are larger than life/have a lot of energy, and some people may not know how to handle that.' She will probably ask what you mean, and you can then offer some examples that make clear how overbearing she can be. You can't change her, but you may make her a little more self-aware.

With a child
In this case, the goal often isn't to spare his feelings but to reassure him. Answer typical questions – where do people go when they die? – directly, if simply, as the situation requires. If you don't know the answer, say so. Consider his age and the nature of his queries. If you're a parent whose child is questioning the existence of Santa Claus or the Easter Bunny, try to gauge whether he's asking because he really wants to know the real deal or he wants you to protect him from it; then give him exactly what he is looking for. The child will almost always let you know when he's ready for the next version in these situations. When it comes to more serious issues, such as the death of a family member, level with the child using language that's gentle and appropriate. Though it may be difficult, tell the truth in these instances, because kids can smell a lie, and they learn the value of honesty from you.

> 'Keep your facts, I'm going with the truth.'
>
> – Stephen Colbert, author and humorist

Meditate

Meditation isn't what you may think. For starters, it doesn't have to involve anything esoteric or removed from day-to-day life. According to Sharon Salzberg, author and teacher of meditation practices: 'It's really just skills training in concentration, mindfulness and compassion. It allows us to steady, refine and open our powers of attention.' The benefits are proven: meditation can help curb pain, lessen the effects of stress, anxiety and depression; and improve memory and learning. Studies have also shown that people who meditate are generally calmer and happier than people who don't. And they sleep better, too.

Get in the mood

Wear comfortable clothing – something that isn't going to tug or constrict you. If you're sitting in a chair, put your feet on the floor. If you're sitting on the floor, make sure it's in a position you can comfortably sustain. Let your hands rest easily in your lap. Relax your shoulders, and lift your chest. Eyes open or eyes closed? Your call.

Breathe

Meditation instructor Nancy O'Hara advises students to 'Just breathe. Expect nothing.' After just one or two breaths, your mind is going to race in 10 directions – the list you have to write, the shopping you need to get, what colour to paint the bedroom. But don't get frustrated. According to Salzberg, this is the key to meditation: acknowledge your lapse in concentration, then 'let go of what has distracted you, and simply begin again.'

Breathe in, then breathe out, taking as long to inhale as to exhale. Try to isolate your awareness to this single thing: your breathing. Repeating a particular word or phrase can help with focus. You can say a favourite line of poetry, even 'I breathe in; I breathe out.' As you settle into a rhythm, you become more aware of being in the moment, and your body begins to move to a state of calm.

Take time out

Some teachers say you should meditate at the same hour and for the same amount of time every day in the same place. If that's easy for you to accomplish, great. But if it's going to add to your stress level, you don't have to take the structured approach. If you have only a random minute here or there throughout the day, take it. If you have five minutes, even better.

What's the best relaxation advice you've ever heard?

Do better...

There are skills that few ever master – like negotiating peace in the Middle East. But then, unless you're secretary of state, who really has the need? It's those other talents we could make excellent use of if only we had them. Talents like making a memorable toast, getting a kite aloft or fending off an onerous task with finesse. Nothing monumental, but how much sweeter would life be if we could do better at any of them? The following compendium of tips is aimed at showing how easy it is to **DO BETTER** at life's small challenges – and how big the payoffs can be.

89

Get great seats

Why does everyone else end up with Centre Court seats at Wimbledon, tickets for the FA Cup final or in the front row to hear U2 at the O2 when you can't even snag a stool at the bar in your local pub to watch it on TV? No doubt these people are rich enough to buy those premium seats from a broker, lucky enough to wind up with tickets from their brother-in-law's boss's boss or know a few tricks that you don't. So if super-rich or well connected doesn't describe you, here are a few ways to nab the best seats.

Join a club

When you join a particular team's or performer's fan club, you are often given first crack at the best seats for their events, usually before tickets are available to the general public. Sign up to receive newsletters, event notices and any other exclusive information the club may give out, as this will no doubt put you first in line when the schedule is announced.

Be patient

When hunting online for tickets, 'don't look and leave', says Joellen Ferrer of StubHub.com. Inventory is constantly changing, so keep checking back to see which seats or dates may have opened up. As the event nears, the venue or event producer is likely to make more seats available.

Search more than one site

Savvy ticket hunters know the importance of tapping every online resource to find the best seats and prices. If you want to weigh as many options as are out there, check sites such as StubHub UK, Gumtree and eBay – all at once – in order to comparison shop. Also take a look at Stereoboard.com, a ticket comparison search engine that helps music fans to locate tickets for more than 25,000 gigs and events from trusted sellers and official outlets, even for sold-out events.

WHAT'S A GOOD SEAT? Every venue is different, but these rules of thumb can help you avoid sitting behind a pillar at that West End show. Stay toward the centre of any of the middle sections to ensure a direct view. The orchestra section is best, although the first circle of a larger theatre can be nice, too, and it's usually preferable to the back of the orchestra. If you can't secure a seat in rows A to M, look in the front rows of the next level up. Generally, the view, acoustics, and general ambience are not ideal in seats that are located under an upper section.

Say no

When the head asks if you wouldn't mind running the school jumble sale or your work colleague pleads with you to take over his project while he's on holiday, it's easy – not to mention nice – to agree to help out. What's hard is following through when you've also got to pick up the car at the garage, post your mother a birthday present and check in on a sick friend. The solution is to say no. Firmly, politely and without resentment. The trick? Keep it short. Here's what really works.

'No, but thank you for asking.'
This one is genius. He's asking the favour, but *you* thank *him* for thinking of you as you firmly close the door. It works with just about any kind of request, and the asker rarely knows how to respond.

'I'd love to, but I simply can't make that big a commitment. Is there another way I could help out?'
Here you're making it crystal clear that you aren't available for the task being pressed upon you but that you're not completely brushing off the person in need, either. No one can hate you when you're offering to lend a hand elsewhere.

'I'm not able to take that on right now.'
This is code for 'I do not have room in my life for it, and if I took it on, not only would it not get done, I'd probably end up going completely mad.' It's as much about levelling with yourself as it is with the person asking.

'No, but I bet so-and-so can help you.'
This is a solid no, with a generous side of helpfulness. And think of all the wonderful people you can recommend in your place! (If it's a particularly onerous chore, be sure to suggest your meddlesome neighbour.)

'I'm really not OK with that.'

Sometimes it's all right to use your no to set the record straight about your position, especially when the request goes against your values. 'I'm afraid I don't support that cause/candidate/ organisation.'

BUT FIRST SAY YES Author and business journalist Suzy Welch has looked closely at the career and quality-of-life costs of saying yes *and* no. She recommends saying yes as much as possible when you're young to gain experience and then putting that valuable goodwill in the bank for the future. Over time, as life priorities take shape, you can start saying no – carefully and strategically – so that what you're doing with your time reflects how you want to live your life. We also like Welch's 10-10-10 rule: for every decision, ask yourself how you're likely to feel after 10 minutes, 10 months and 10 years.

Let go of stuff

The things we use in our daily lives were once made to last a lifetime. Today, it's a disposable, recyclable, replaceable world. Nappies, contact lenses, razors, pens, even mobile phones – we use them and toss them. But some things we can hang on to for too long – from relationships to clothing, leftovers and toasters. Here's when it is time to let go of...

Your favourite pair of old jeans

Sure, they represent the hopefulness (or hotness) of your youth. But here's the cold, hard truth: if they've been more than two sizes too small for more than five years, you're unlikely to wear them again. And having your 'skinny jeans' stare at you from your closet for eternity will just depress you. Should you happen to work your way down to that size again, surely you will deserve a new pair of jeans.

Tax and other financial documents

Think you can throw away all your paperwork now that nearly every financial document you have is available virtually? Not so fast. The Inland Revenue requires records dating back five more years after the normal filing deadline of 31 January. This date applies even if you've sent in a paper tax return. If HMRC sent you – or you sent back – your tax return very late, or if a check into your return has been started, you may need to keep your records for longer. Mortgage lenders usually want at least a 12-month history of your finances, so holding on to the previous year's banking and savings statements – plus payslips and credit card bills – is a good idea. For ID purposes, utility bills, council tax payments and phone records from the past six months might be useful. Keep every document related to your mortgage and car loans, at least until the loans are satisfied.

Medicine and suncare products

Chuck all over-the-counter and prescription drugs in accordance with the expiry date. While a painkiller, antibiotic or cough medicine can retain its potency after this time, it can also degrade into an unsafe or ineffective product. Take any medicines back to your pharmacist, who can dispose of them for you. Sunscreen loses its effectiveness over time. Check the expiry dates – a new bottle generally lasts for two to three years.

Household appliances

Should you keep a bulky household appliance or get a new one? The key is how you use it. The average life of an appliance is 10 to 15 years, but a big family that is rough on one can cut that life expectancy down by a lot. If you take good care of the appliance, though, it can last for 20 years, so the minor repairs you may need along the way would be worth it. There have been a lot of improvements in appliances over the last decade or so, but that doesn't necessarily translate to longer life. If you need a significant repair and the machine shows a lot of use and abuse, it may be worth putting the cost towards buying new on rather than paying out for a costly repair.

Food

The short answer is: 'When in doubt, throw it out.' More specifically, toss any meat, poultry or other leftovers cooked more than two days earlier, deeply dented cans, jars with bulging lids or anything with freezer burn. Don't use any food or drink after the end of the 'use by' date on the label, even if it looks and smells fine. Using it after this date could put your health at risk. If a food can be frozen its life can be extended beyond the 'use by' date. But make sure you follow any instructions on the pack, such as 'cook from frozen' or 'defrost thoroughly'.

'Best before' dates are about quality, not safety. When the date is passed, it doesn't mean that the food will make you ill, but the taste and texture may not be as good. Eggs can be eaten a day or two after their 'best before' date, but must be cooked thoroughly. Every year in the UK we throw away 7.2 million tonnes of food and drink, much of which could have been eaten, so don't automatically sling out food that is past its 'best before' date. And of course, the date will only be accurate if the food has been stored according to the instructions on the label.

Your kids' artwork

This one's a heartbreaker. But let's face it; you can't keep it all. And not every little darling is a Degas in the making. At the end of the school year, pick one or two pieces you can't imagine living without and frame them.

WHERE TO BIN THE THINGS YOU CAN'T JUST BIN

▶▶ **Batteries** Neither single-use batteries nor rechargeable ones should be thrown out with the regular rubbish. To find a disposal centre in your area, go to recyclenow.com and use the recycling bank locator to find your nearest recycling facilities, or contact your local authority.

▶▶ **Lightbulbs** Incandescent bulbs should go in with your regular waste, but energy-saving bulbs need to be disposed of through your town's local waste and recycling centre, found by contacting your local council.

▶▶ **Computers** Some companies offer a service where you can return your old computer for nothing – ask before you buy. If not, your council may run a scheme (but might charge for collection). Alternatively, the Freecycle Network (freecycle.org) will help you give away your old machine and Computer Aid International sends computers to developing countries.

▶▶ **Household chemicals** Protocol for the disposal of paint cans, turpentine, pest control products and other chemicals varies locally, so check with your local council for information about where and how to get rid of potentially toxic household chemicals.

Resolve to let go of five things.

How to avoid
a ticket

First you hear the siren and see the flashing lights in your rearview mirror. Then you check the dashboard to calculate how far over the limit you were speeding and how much money – and points – this is going to set you back. Unless you were going 70 in a 30mph zone while schoolchildren were crossing the road, you probably have room for negotiation. More often than not, your offence isn't the only factor in play. The traffic officer's monthly ticket quota and his mood may also determine your fate. Here's how to coax him into going easy on you.

Make a good impression

Many officers decide whether you're going to get a ticket before they approach your vehicle. So it's advisable to keep your car clean and tidy, and to forgo spoilers and tinted windows. You want to look responsible and law abiding rather than anarchic.'

Be ready to talk

Usually the police officer takes a minute or two before coming over to your car to ask for your licence and registration. Take advantage of that time by preparing what you are going to say. A ticket that's already been written out is pretty much cast in stone. If you have something to say that you think might make a difference, tell the officer right away, because once he starts writing the ticket, he can't just tear it up.

Don't admit you were speeding

If you do get pulled over, says a former police officer, never acknowledge that you were speeding. You don't want to give the police any ammunition against you. Admitting guilt at the roadside will condemn you to defeat in court. When an officer claims you were speeding, give a brief, non-committal response such as, 'I see,' or 'I was not aware of my speed'. Deal with the police as quickly and politely as possible. You don't want them to remember anything about you, except that you did as you were told.

Don't push it

If you know you're guilty, it's probably best to accept the situation, pay your fixed penalty fine (plus points) and move on. Fighting a lost cause through the legal system can be both expensive and fruitless. Or you could ask if you can take road-safety tuition as an alternative to penalty points. When the ticket carries the risk of a ban, it's best to seek legal advice if you want to stay on the road, although logging onto the website speed-trap.co.uk may help. If you plan to contest charges, make notes at the scene to keep your evidence as accurate as that of the prosecution.

Wave at lurking police cars

If you're driving a little faster than you should be and spot a police vehicle, it might help if you wave politely, says a former police officer. The policeman may either think that you know each other and wave back, or else that you're acknowledging your error and are letting him know that you're slowing down.

Do better...

GET THE CHARGES DROPPED? Most motorists don't contest speeding tickets, but there are circumstances in which they possibly could. If, due to local authority negligence, speed limits are not clearly posted or signs are obscured, you could appeal. When a speed limit has recently been changed and no clear notice has been given, a court might accept an appeal if you didn't exceed the previous limit. If you are caught by a speed camera, the police must send you a Notice of Intended Prosecution within 14 days for a subsequent charge to be valid. If they don't meet this deadline, it's not.

Fly a **kite**

That song from *Mary Poppins* makes it sound so easy, but most of us who haven't done it in a while are more like Charlie Brown, with our kite stubbornly hugging the ground or catching in a tree. And yet the swoosh you hear when a kite first lifts in the air, the tug of the string when it's finally in flight, the snap of the tail in the wind – it takes you right back to the simple joy you felt as a child with your gaze up in the clouds. Luckily, kites are more user-friendly and reliable than ever. The flimsy paper-and-sticks frame of the 1950s has given way to sleeker variations made of polyester sailcloth and carbon rods. Today getting the thing airborne is, well, a breeze, but there are a few simple tips that make flying the kite even easier, and safer for you and others around you.

Ditch the diamond

Diamonds are the classic shape. With only two or three parts to assemble, they are easy to set up but are aerodynamically undesirable. Instead, go with parafoil, or sled, kites which have cells that inflate in the wind, much like a windsock. They are very stable and great for any skill level.

Choose a wide-open space

Avoid areas where the wind is blocked by buildings or trees, and steer clear of those with power lines. The beach is picturesque, but the kite could land in the water. Your best bet is a large open field with unobstructed wind.

Launch it like a pro

It may be fun and a bit of an aerobic workout to grab the string and run madly into the wind to send your kite aloft, but it's not the best method. Instead, have a companion hold the kite or lean it against a post or tree. Then do what is called a long line launch. Walk 30 metres into the wind while letting the string out on the ground. Gently pull the kite out of your friend's hand, and it should soar instantly. Remember that the kite can only head skyward *against* the wind, not *with* the wind. The optimum wind speeds for flying a kite are between 13 and 32 kilometres per hour.

KITE CENTRAL Long Beach, Washington, USA is home to the World Kite Museum and Hall of Fame, which has honoured such devotees as Wilbur and Orville Wright, who used kites to experiment with human-powered flight; Paul Garber, a kite collector whose historic collection can be seen at the Smithsonian Institution in Washington, D.C.; and a fellow known simply as the First Kite Flyer, who is believed to have lived in China in the fourth century B.C. The Washington State International Kite Festival takes place every August at Long Beach, drawing famous competitive kite flyers from around the world, as well as tens of thousands of kite-loving spectators.

Do better...

Entertain a child

'Hell is other people,' Jean-Paul Sartre once wrote, but in truth, hell is other people's children, particularly when those children are sitting near you on a transcontinental flight or in a waiting room, both of which seem to have been designed to encourage screeching, seat kicking and other forms of misbehaviour. Before lending him your iPhone to play Bubble Breaker (complete with annoying sound effects) or showing him how to master a game of coin rugby on the tray table (while you work on your laptop in the 'end zone'), put your fellow sufferers out of their misery with these kid-pleasing tricks.

The old 'Can you help me?' ploy
A child is often delighted to be asked for help, even if you don't really need it. Give the youngster your business cards and ask her to count them for you or to make them all go the same way or to put them in/take them out of an envelope. Take out a piece of paper and pencil and tell her you need to find a fairy princess/circus pony/dandelion, but you don't know what it looks like – could she draw one for you? Or flip through a magazine with her and ask her to help you find all the pictures with something red in them.

The never-ending word game
Psychologist Carl Jung gave us word association to bring to light our deepest thoughts and feelings; comic troupe Monty Python gave us Word Association Football to keep us from throttling each other on long trips. The rules are simple: you say a word or phrase, the other person repeats it and then adds another word or phrase, and so on. Include verbs, adjectives and adverbs to build a story; play with homonyms (use *axe* instead of *acts, metal* instead of *mettle*). Soon you will have constructed the world's most ridiculous Frankenstein monster of a

sentence/paragraph/story. Keep it simple and silly for a little one, or let the creative juices flow with a bigger kid. Of course, you can just say it out loud, but it's best to write it down as you go so you can really appreciate the whole absurd concoction. For inspiration, check out John Cleese's 'Word Association' piece on the Python classic 1975 recording *Matching Tie & Handkerchief*. Here's a snippet:

> So on the button, my contention causing all the headaches, is that unless we take into account of Monte Cristo in our thinking George the Fifth this phenomenon the other hand we shall not be able satisfact or fiction section of the Watford Public Library againily to understand to attention when I'm talking to you and stop laughing, about human nature, man's psychological make-up some story the wife'll believe and hence the very meaning of life...

String figures

If you have an 80cm loop of string handy (and really, who doesn't?), you can use it like this to charm and delight kids as long as you know how to use it. Start by demonstrating on the child's hands (see diagram, opposite) before letting him attempt the trick himself. And if you're lucky, he'll learn how to do it, keep the string and show his brother the game while you get back to the in-flight movie. Of the hundreds of string figures to be learned, Cat's Cradle is one of the easiest. For more ideas, visit Squidoo.com/string-games.

What's your child's favourite game?

CAT'S CRADLE

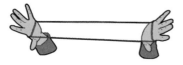

1. Slip your hands through the loop of string and pull them apart until the string is taut. Wind the string once around each of your palms.

2. Slip one middle finger through the loop on the opposite palm and pull your hands apart. Repeat with the other hand to form a 'cat's cradle'.

3. Have your new little friend pinch the crisscrosses in the string with her thumb and forefinger.

4. Next, have her pull the strings outwards.

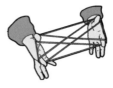

5. Then down and back under the sides of your cat's cradle, coming up through the centre.

6. Now she lifts the string off your hands and pulls her own fingers and hands apart to create a new shape called 'the soldier's bed'.

Beat the house

Lady Luck makes unscheduled appearances – at work, in sports, in romance. But most people go looking for her at her best-known address: the casino.

'There are a lot of happy faces on the plane trip to Vegas. People think they're going to win enough money to pay the mortgage and send the kids to college,' says Simon Lovell, author of *How to Cheat at Everything.* And on the trip back home? A lot of sad, tired faces. 'I came out to Vegas in a $45,000 Jaguar,' goes the very old joke, 'and I left in a half-million-dollar bus.' According to Lovell, it doesn't have to be that way. It's a question of understanding what you're up against. 'There are runs where the game will go in your favour. That's just how life is. And there are runs when the game will go against you. That's how life is, too.'

So if I get 22, is that better than 21?

Don't play a game you don't know, and never play anything without knowing all the rules. Don't fall prey to nonsense when it comes to placing bets. For example, says Lovell, 'ignore those roulette boards that tell you what numbers have gone before. The roulette ball has no memory.' And never play the slots. 'There's a reason they call them one-armed bandits,' he says. 'They make more money than every game in the casino combined. People will tell you slots pay out 95 per cent. OK, but think about it: if someone came up to you and said, 'Give me a dollar and I'll give you 95 cents,' you'd think he was crazy.'

Beat the system – a little

Go to the casino bar and pop a pound into a slot machine. Because you're playing the machine, chances are you'll be offered a free drink. If you win, great, it's found money. If you've lost your money, on the other hand, you've still managed to get a Bloody Mary at a very appealing discount.

Manage your money

Think of the tab for a nice night out with your spouse and bring that exact amount – in cash – to the tables. Never, *ever* bring along a debit or credit card. Tuck any winnings into your left pocket and do not touch them. If there's something in your pocket at the end of the night, congratulations – you got lucky. If your pocket is empty, well, you're out no more than the cost of that nice evening out.

When the chips are down...

There's a reason casino carpeting has a busy pattern: it's to keep your eyes up so you can look straight ahead to the array of gaming tables. Well, lower your eyes and have a look around. You'll often see chips and bills that people have unwittingly dropped. Hoover them up.

Throw in the towel

If you're suddenly up £200 or £2,000, it's probably the end of your good luck, not the beginning, cautions Lovell: 'When you're up, walk away. The more time you spend at the tables, the more likely you are to have your money disappear.'

That goes double if you're down a large wad; in which case, run – don't walk – away. Not convinced this is the best advice? Rent the classic Albert Brooks movie, *Lost in America,* and watch the scene about 'the nest egg'.

Bargain
down anything

We love coupons, discounts and big sales. Haggling? Not so much. But the guy who's comfortable bartering gets the better deal. Here's how to get over your squeamishness and bargain for the price you want.

Home appliances and electronics

The best times to negotiate are just as the shop opens or right before closing, says Tiffany Aliche, author of *The One-Week Budget.* Ask to speak to the manager, who is bound to be more accessible at the beginning or the end of the day than in the middle, when things are busy. Explain that you're ready to buy right here, right now, and name your price. Don't be too surprised if he bites; a fast sale to open or close the day can be highly motivating to the person who's on the hook for store sales volume.

Food

Forage beyond the supermarket. At a local farmer's produce stand, if you say you're willing to buy in volume (and are ready to do some serious pickling or have extra room in the freezer), you can almost certainly push down the price. An hour or two before closing time, gourmet shops often mark down prepared foods and salad-bar items.

Dental work

Dentists aren't just running a practice; they're also running a business. Ask for a discount before you have a procedure. Some of them will give you a small price break if you pay what you owe all at once or if you offer to pay in cash.

Do better...

Home improvements

Call contractors in the winter, when business is typically slow. When they quote a price for a job, ask for a 10 per cent discount. See what kind of deal you can get by replacing your 30-year-old boiler in the middle of July.

Cable or satellite television

Call your provider and say its service is too expensive and you want to cancel immediately. Go ahead; be indignant. The cable representative will most likely offer you a lower price. Don't jump at it. Instead, say that's still too expensive and ask for an even lower price. If you're offered a *really* great rate, ask that it be extended for 12 months beyond the standard contract – or forever.

Online purchases

If you find a better price at Web Store B but want to take advantage of the free-shipping deal at Web Store A, call Web Store A's customer service department or speak with the live-chat representative online to request a price match. And before you buy anywhere on the web, ask someone at the company if there's a discount code or a coupon you can use. Or visit a site like Myvouchercodes.co.uk or Promocodes.co.uk.

TOO HIGH! Best-selling author and world traveller Timothy Ferris learned plenty about bargaining on a trip to India, where the marketplaces are renowned for aggressive and sophisticated haggling. His experience taught him to aim high and not be shy. Ask for 70 per cent off, and settle for nothing less than 30 per cent. Make them work for the sale. Ask to see lots of merchandise so the vendor will have invested time in the transaction and be less inclined to let you walk away. Say 'Too high!' as often as necessary to keep the negotiation moving in your direction. Focus your haggling on one item, but be prepared to ask if the seller will give you a better deal if you purchase two.

What's the best deal you ever got?

Do better...

Get through to a real
live person

'Thank you for calling. We appreciate your business and look forward to assisting you. Please press 1 for billing. Press 2 for tech support. Press 3 for new orders. Press 4 for existing orders. Press 5 to track your order. Press 6 to repeat this menu. Press 7 for more options. Press 8 if you really believe you're ever going to get to talk to a real live person.'

Ah, the automated call centre, where the wait is long, the frustration high and the recorded music cheesy. Here's how to dial S for satisfaction.

Hold the phone

Before you even think of picking up the phone, try the self-serve options on the company's website. Companies want to help you help yourself, whether it's locating a store, finding out the hours of operation, downloading a driver or cancelling a flight. Also check out websites like GetHuman.com, which lists phone numbers, call-centre shortcuts and average wait times for hundreds of companies, among them airlines, banks and cable operators, or try Saynoto0870.com.

Zero in

Depending on the call centre, hitting 0 or bellowing 'operator' can speed your journey to a live voice, says Patrick Gray, a communication systems consultant. Another option: press absolutely nothing. 'If you don't select an option, many systems will assume you have a rotary phone and automatically route you to an operator,' he says. But when you want tech support, don't press the number for billing (thinking you stand a good chance of getting a human being who will take your money). The employee who's equipped to process your credit card will probably be unable to transfer you to the right place and you will have to call back and start the whole process again.

Make a smart call

Spend a few minutes trying to understand the company you're trying to reach. If, for example, you need to talk to your airline about changes in a trip that's two months away and you notice there's a blizzard in the carrier's major hub, wait until the storm has passed to make the call. Similarly, don't try to get through during a call centre's peak hours. Waiting times will be far shorter if you call first thing in the morning, and after 9 P.M. can work well for a 24-hour call centre, as can weekends.

Broadcast your frustration

If a company has a frustrating phone menu or the service has not been adequate (poor communication and an inability to deviate from the script are among the most common complaints), share your displeasure on Twitter or Facebook. 'It may not help you right at the moment, but it will down the road,' says Berger. 'Companies feel the viral impact of bad service much more quickly these days.'

Win an **argument**

Just once, you'd like to have the right ammo to prevail in an argument with your spouse, your teen or your work colleague. Being able to change someone's perspective is a terrifically useful skill, but change isn't generally what we're after in the heat of battle. 'When it's all about winning rather than actually getting our point across in an argument, all that happens is we alienate people,' says Kevin Dutton, a psychologist and the author of *Split Second Persuasion*. Here are ways to prevail while preserving the peace.

Use persuasive body language

Make eye contact with your opponent while keeping in mind that you're trying to win an argument, not a staring contest. If your adversary crosses his legs when talking to you, wait a few seconds (so it doesn't seem obvious or mocking) and cross *your* legs in the same fashion. If he leans forward or sits back, again, wait briefly and then follow suit. 'This 'mirroring' will make your adversary feel more sympathetic to you and your point of view. People like people who seem like themselves,' says Dutton. When you're making a point, a quick touch on your opponent's arm can have a similarly positive effect. So can holding hands when your sparring partner is your spouse.

Just stick to the facts

Having a debate about global warming or the role of NATO? Make sure your mind is loaded with facts before you shoot off your mouth. The same goes for more mundane domestic matters. If, for example, you and your spouse are rowing about household finances, saying 'You're a horrible money manager' is no way to carry the day, says Lauren Meckler, a life coach. It's a subjective claim rather than an objective one. Instead, be ready with a fact-based position: 'Because you didn't make the deposit last week, a cheque bounced. This has happened three times in the last two months. I think I should take over the money management.' When your child questions his midnight curfew, stick to the facts. Explain that his preferred 2 A.M. return will wake you up, which is not a good thing, since you have an early meeting. Say, 'I'm letting you know you have to be home at 12 o'clock. You can argue and not go at all, or accept my conditions and have a great time until midnight.' Jay Heinrichs, author of *Thank You for Arguing*, also urges a change in tenses. Talking about who was to blame is dealing with the past. Shift to the future: how will this keep us from spending more money? How will this keep the toilet lid down?

Tune in to your tone

How you argue is key. 'Use an adult, non-accusatory tone. Think monotone,' says Meckler. 'The more charged you sound, the more you discredit yourself.' And manage your emotions. If, in the thick of an argument, you're having a negative reaction, acknowledge it, then say, 'I'm getting really angry. I'm going to leave the room.' Exit, take a walk around the block, calm down, come back and resume the debate.

ARGUING HAS A BAD REP 'People mistake arguing for fighting,' explains Heinrichs. In fact, he says, a successful argument sustains relationships and persuades other people to make the decision you want them to make. 'They also mistake arguing for overwhelming the other person with logic. It's not about scoring a victory; it's about setting a goal and meeting it,' says Heinrichs. And whether it's a who's-to-blame argument or a values argument, 'if it turns into a fight, you are almost certainly not going to get what you want.'

Have a great time
at a party

Show me a child who doesn't want to go to a party and I'll show you a child who's coming down with the flu. Children don't worry about having a ready, steady stream of small talk. They don't fret about being commandeered by a boor or a bore. They don't keep looking at their watch, wondering when they can beat a path to the exit. And when children start to misbehave at a party, someone takes them by the hand, thanks the host for the goody bags and buckles them into their car seat to make a swift getaway. Well, you're an adult now, and while parties may not be as much fun as they used to be, the social stakes are a little higher. Here's how to avoid party pain and get more party pleasure.

The right frame of mind

If you're counting on a party to be dull, dull is what it will be. Go with positive expectations, and the gathering will be, if not necessarily a rocking good one, a perfectly pleasant way to spend a few hours. How the event unfolds is up to you. See yourself having fun and you'll most likely have fun, too. It really is as simple as that.

Um, uh, er...

There is always that anxious moment when you walk into a party and realise that you do not see a single familiar face. Before you grab your coat and sneak back out the door, consider that your fellow merrymakers are quite possibly in the same lonely boat. Be the person who starts the conversations and puts others at ease. If that's not your style, simply acknowledge your dilemma. Approach the friendly-looking person or group and say, 'I confess I don't know a soul. May I join you? I'm _____. And you are?' And now you know someone.

Let's talk about you

The best strategy to get – and keep – a conversation going is to ask questions. People never tire of talking about themselves and are immediately enchanted by anyone who expresses interest. Make sure your questions are open-ended – ones that can't simply be answered with a yes or a no but instead need some explanation or that lead seamlessly to another. If you stick to this simple rule, you'll see how easily the conversation flows. Question: 'Where are you from?' Answer: 'I moved here from Manchester two years ago.' Now you can start asking about Manchester, which should certainly keep you busy for the next 10 minutes, maybe an hour. It also allows you to bring others into the conversation easily. 'Oh, Tom. Simon just told me he's from Manchester. Aren't you a big Man Utd fan?' You party animal.

Exit strategy

If you've learned everything you care to know about someone, it's time to move on to chat with another guest. Here are some polite ways to extricate yourself:

▸▸ *'I see my friend Sue just arrived. I'm going to go say hello. I really enjoyed talking with you!'*

▸▸ *'I see my friend Sue, and I'd love to introduce you.' Then after they're chatting, excuse yourself to get a drink and slip away into the crowd.*

▸▸ *'Excuse me a minute. I'm going to try to catch my friend Sue before she leaves.'*

UNHAPPY TALK There are 10 subjects you should avoid talking about at a party if you really want to ensure that everyone has a good time. They are politics and religion, of course. Also, how smart/talented/gifted/beautiful your child is. How smart/talented/gifted/adorable your pet is. How much something cost you. Your physical ailments. Your sex life. The broken stuff in your house. Gossip. And things you hate – because, really, who wants to know?

Look your best in
every photo

Is it starting to strike people as strange that the only picture of you in the family album is the one taken just after you were born? Does everyone find those jokes about the camera stealing your soul a bit stale? Get over it. It's absolutely true that some people are more photogenic than others, according to fashion photographer Diane Vasil. But even those whom the camera doesn't love can make the most of what they have. When you need a good photo of yourself for work, a family reunion or a social networking site, these tips will do just the trick.

Position yourself perfectly

Don't drop your chin; it makes you look as though you've misplaced your neck. Don't tilt your head up too far unless you want a wallet-size shot of your nostrils. And don't cock it to the side 'because it just makes you look dumb and your cheek look saggy,' Vasil says bluntly. Stand with your legs a few inches apart, or pose with one crossed over the other. 'It makes them look better,' she says, adding that another option – standing sideways, head turned towards the camera – can make you look thinner. To avoid a shot that looks too stiff and posed, lean on a chair or a couch. And instead of letting your hands dangle, put them on your hips or cross them in front of you.

Check the light

If you're being photographed outside, try to schedule the session early in the morning or late in the day, when the light is most flattering, suggests photographer David Johnson. Or try standing in front of the shady side of a building, which will offer a softer light, he says.

Dress right

Wear that one thing in your wardrobe that always makes you feel attractive, says Vasil. Avoid colours that are close to your skin tone, such as pastel pink, beige or brown – they can wash you out. And pass up busy patterns, stripes and spots, which can be distracting. For women, a crisp white button-down blouse is preferable to a white T-shirt. For men, Johnson recommends layering a jacket or V-neck sweater over a collared shirt to 'add some geometry and interest to the shot'.

Size up your face

Models are well aware of how their features play from different angles. Take a good long look in the mirror to see which side of your face looks better. You can also learn a thing or two by playing with self-photo programmes on your computer, camera software or smartphone, or have someone photograph you from different vantage points to figure out your 'good side' – and remember it the next time someone comes at you with a Leica.

Skip the cheese

'Better to laugh rather than say cheese,' says Vasil. 'You'll get a more natural grin.' Another way to ensure a fresh, authentic expression: just before the picture is snapped, look away, then quickly look back while breaking into a smile.

What is your favourite photo, and where was it taken?

Spot trends

Crystal balls and soothsayers are hard to come by. Tea leaves, tarot cards and pig entrails are notoriously unreliable as tools of prognostication. But there are some surefire ways to predict the future – not necessarily whether you'll win the lottery but what the next hot trend will be, says Ann Mack, the director of trend spotting at JWT, one of the world's largest advertising agencies.

Get curious

Mack advises that you read as much as you can – and get as many viewpoints as you can. 'People tend to simply look at things that confirm what they already believe,' she says. 'Spotting trends requires taking information from disparate sources and connecting dots that don't necessarily seem to connect. If you're not reading everything you can get your hands on, it's hard to make those connections.'

Check tech

Technology either drives trends or is at the centre of them, according to Mack. For example, she recently identified a new trend she calls Outsource Self-Control after she and her colleagues took note of a BlackBerry app that keeps you from sending or receiving texts or emails if you're driving, as well as a device that shuts off your iPhone. A little more research showed a pattern of policing ourselves with our own technology.

Look to the past

It may be trite, but it's true: history repeats itself. During a recession, for example, people buy more small pleasures, like chocolates (because, of course, people can't afford big pleasures). Similarly, during the dot-com bust of 2000, there was a jump in lipstick purchases, perhaps as compensation for the big-ticket beauty and fashion items that were suddenly out of reach. 'You can anticipate certain things,' says Mack, 'because they *always* happen during a down or boom period.'

Go to extremes

Whenever a trend goes too far in one direction, there's bound to be a backlash. If women are wearing man-tailored suits one year, bet that an ultrafeminine look will be next year's style. Likewise, now that technology is becoming as integral to our lives as food and clothing, there's a movement afoot to encourage people to log off, hang up and power down to improve languishing relationships.

FOUR TRENDS NO ONE PREDICTED While arming yourself with knowledge will give you a leg up when it comes to spotting the next big thing, keep in mind that some revolutionary ideas weren't the result of R&D. Here, from Uphaa.com, are a few their inventors simply stumbled across.

▸▸ **Post-its** Back in 1970, Spencer Silver, a researcher for 3M, was beating his head against a wall. He had been trying to formulate a new extra-strong adhesive but had so far only managed to create one that wouldn't *stay* glued to anything. Fast-forward four years, when Arthur Fry, a 3M colleague and member of Silver's church choir, finds himself constantly annoyed that the paper bookmarks he uses in his hymnal are always falling out. Then the lightbulb pops on. He recalls Silver's adhesive, applies it to his bookmarks, and an office-supply legend is born.

▸▸ **Vaseline** In 1869, Robert Chesebrough went to work in the oilfields of Pennsylvania, where he discovered that a thick, waxy substance that formed on the drills was the bane of the roughnecks' existence. They complained it gummed up their equipment and slowed them down, though when it came to small cuts, they said, the stuff worked to speed up the healing process. Intrigued, Chesebrough took a sample of the wax back to his laboratory in Brooklyn, and soon he was selling a jar a minute of the stuff, which he dubbed Vaseline (from *Wasser*, the German for 'water,' and *elaion*, Greek for 'oil').

▶ **Microwave oven** Before there were appliances that zapped ready meals, microwaves were part of what made radar possible during the war; the devices that produced them were called magnetrons. In 1945, Percy Lebaron Spencer, an American engineer and inventor, was standing by a functioning magnetron when he noticed that the chocolate bar in his pocket had melted. After realising it was the microwaves that had caused the goo, he went on to conduct experiments that eventually led to the first microwave oven, which weighed about 340kg and was nearly the size of a refrigerator.

▶ **Velcro** One day when George de Mestral, a Swiss engineer, got home from a hunting trip in the Alps, he noticed that both he and his dog were covered in burrs. He plucked one from his coat and placed it under a microscope, which revealed that the tiny seed sac was covered in hooked strands, which had caught in the tiny loops of fabric on his coat. By re-creating such hooks and loops, Mestral was able to devise the fastening system known as Velcro (derived from *velour* and *crochet*). More than 50 years later, it has held together everything from trainers to a human heart during the first artificial heart surgery. As Mestral later told his former bosses at work, 'If any of your employees ask for a two-week holiday to go hunting, say yes.'

What trends do you predict?

Avoid
jet lag

If it's Tuesday, this must be... yawn. It's great to rack up frequent-flyer miles, but it's not so pleasant to experience the bodily toll of zipping from Bangor to Bangalore, Luton to Latvia. Pills can help, of course, but we like the natural way:

1. *Eat (but don't overeat) starches like pasta or rice the night before you fly across more than two time zones. Carbs help your body adjust more quickly to sudden jolts to its circadian rhythms.*

2. *The air circulating in the cabin during flight tends to be bone dry, which causes dehydration, a big contributor to jet lag. Avoid making things worse – pass up the caffeine and alcohol (the latter is two to three times more dehydrating than usual when consumed at cruising altitude). And drink lots of water before, during and after your flight.*

3. *If you're flying at night, sleep. Use earplugs and an eye mask, turn down the lights, cover up and adjust your air-conditioning valve to a cool setting, which sends a message to your body that it's night-time.*

4. *Switch your watch to local time before getting off the plane.*

5. *Resist the urge to nap on arrival, no matter how tired you are. If you're landing in the morning, take a shower and eat eggs for breakfast – the protein will help you through the first day. Then head out right away. Later in the day, try to jog or swim, which will help you fall asleep naturally.*

> ‘One of the advantages of my line of work was that whenever I reached a distant destination, I had to run off the plane and get to work immediately. Generally, I was going on the air a few hours later, often in the middle of the night from a remote airfield in Iraq or a backstreet in Kabul... What I quickly learned is that adrenaline is the best drug for jet lag.’
>
> – Tom Brokaw, NBC commentator and former *Nightly News* anchor

6. *Stay up as late as you can, preferably until your normal bedtime, according to the local clock. And sleep as late as possible the next morning. By that night, you should have successfully tweaked your body's time clock into a new routine.*

Write a **limerick**

There once was a middle-aged man,
An unabashed pro football fan.
With eyes glued to the score,
He could see nothing more,
It's been years since his wife packed and ran.

As anyone familiar with the man from Nantucket knows, a limerick is a five-line poem that features a rhyme scheme of AABBA and offers plenty of opportunity to show off your wit as well as your cheek. No doubt named after the county in Ireland (for reasons that remain murky), the clever little literary concoctions were popularised by Edward Lear in the 1800s. While you may not match Lear's output – he wrote 212 of them – the ability to come up with one is a useful skill at weddings or leaving parties, or whenever the time is right. Here's how.

Find an easy rhyme to start
To begin, it's helpful to think of a subject that has lots of rhymes. 'There once was a dish with an orange' will inevitably lead you nowhere, as you've ended with a word that has no rhyme in English. Play around with the rhymes, going through the alphabet to see what works.

Devise a plot
The first two lines of a limerick establish a premise that the remaining lines complete. In our example, 'middle-aged man' and 'football fan' set up what comes next. How could those two phrases advance both the story and the rhyme?

Ride the rhythm
Limericks have a very distinct metre that seems to hurtle you towards the finish. The first and second lines create a pattern of nine (sometimes eight) stressed and unstressed syllables that

Do better...

sound sort of like this: 'da-DUM da-da-DUM da-da-DUM'. The third and fourth lines follow a five- or six-syllable rhythm, in this case, the latter: 'da-da-DUM da-da-DUM'.

Work towards the climax
With the rhythm of the third and fourth lines in mind, continue with the story. In our example on the left, we have already introduced the man who's a football fan. What kind of drama could come of that?

Wrap it up
The last line should conclude your tale, reinforcing lines three and four. Now read your final version aloud to be sure you've nailed the metre. Sound OK? You're ready for an audience.

Make it a collective effort
Back when people drank sidecars and brandished fondue forks, limericks were second only to Twister as a party highlight. And with everything Don Draper-esque suddenly chic again, you might want to bring back the tradition at your next gathering. With the right crowd, it's simple: the first person offers the first line, the next person adds the second, and so on until you have your whole rhyme. Then the next person starts a new limerick. Continue until someone makes an off-colour reference to the host's wife.

HAIKU, TOO The Japanese verse form of haiku can also provide stylised fun. Nineteenth-century Japanese master Matsuo Basho often focused on the seasons or nature, but modern-day poets can choose anything, as long as they adhere to the rules: a line of five syllables, followed by one of seven, then one of five.

Football fanatic
Cheers loud for the winning team
While misplacing spouse.

Make a great
Halloween costume

Sure, you can go out and buy a rubber *Scream* mask or a naughty nurse costume if you want to look like every other guest at your neighbour's Halloween party (and you'll be waiting for the thumbs up longer than Linus waited for the Great Pumpkin in *Peanuts*). Or you can use your imagination, some odds and ends from around the house, and a few cheap bought items to cook up something frighteningly good.

Be creative

First, abandon all preconceived notions of what a Halloween costume is supposed to be. Frankenstein, witches and ghosts have all been done to death (so to speak). If you want to score points for originality, go as some*thing*, not some*one*. Look around your house for common objects to spark an idea: the bathroom scales, a teapot, your iPad.

Now think about materials you have handy that could help transform you into one of those objects. What about going as a bunch of grapes? Throw on a pair of green pants or tights and a top, cover your torso with purple balloons from a party-supply shop, and you're done. Or maybe you'd rather go as your favourite book. Simply hand-letter two oversize pieces of cardboard, then affix them to your body sandwich board-style. *Voilà!* You're *War and Peace*.

'If human beings genuinely had courage, they'd wear their costumes every day of the year, not just on Halloween.'

– Douglas Coupland, best-selling author

Idioms, clichés and slang can inspire fun, punny costumes. Here's one: cut a few numerals from construction paper, then pin them to your clothing. You're 'Someone You Can Count

On!' Other possibilities include 'All Ears', 'Under the Weather' and 'The Big Cheese'.

Keep it simple

Sometimes the least complicated costumes are the best. Transform yourself into a Jackson Pollock by splattering multicoloured paint across the front of a white sweatshirt and hanging a picture frame around your neck. Become the newest member of Blue Man Group with the help of some blue face paint (see the recipe that follows), a blue latex bald cap, black trousers and a long-sleeved black T-shirt. Your name is William? Draw a big dollar sign on a white T-shirt with a permanent marker and see who can guess: Dollar Bill.

If you're really short on time or money, consider these: dress up as 'blackmail' by wearing all black and putting a postage stamp on your chest. Or tape the front page from an out-of-date newspaper to your shirt. Now you're 'old news'.

FACE IT Armed with a hot glue gun and/or face or body paint, you can whip up more disguises than Inspector Clouseau. To make yourself into Mystique from *X-Men*, for instance, just dress in a snug blue T-shirt and leggings, paint your exposed parts blue and throw on a red wig. Here's what you need to make the paint:

- ➤ 50g (2oz) cornflour

- ➤ 30ml (2tbsp) cold cream (such as Pond's)

- ➤ 30ml (2tbsp) water

- ➤ blue food colouring (several drops)

Mix the ingredients until well blended and apply with a make-up sponge. (You may have to double the recipe if you're covering a lot of skin.) When the night is over, remove with cold cream.

Talk to your doctor

Discussing embarrassing symptoms while wearing a paper gown that offers more ventilation than coverage can make it tempting to say, 'I'm fine' – even when you're not. Get more from your doctor visits not simply by opening your mouth only to say 'Ahhhh', but by describing your symptoms and concerns. Doctors spend an average of 8–10 minutes with each patient. Once you've got an appointment, plan ahead to make sure that you cover everything you want to discuss.

Club med

Bring a list of all prescription and over-the-counter medications you're taking, as well as any alternative medications or supplements, such as vitamins. Better yet, bring the bottles so you can review why and when to take each pill – and what interacts with what.

Where does it hurt?

Don't come in with a laundry list of questions and ailments, because you're not going to leave the office feeling satisfied. This isn't your only shot with the doctor. It's an ongoing relationship, so choose a few things you want to focus on at this particular appointment, write them down and bring them up at the beginning. That way, he doesn't hear 'Oh, by the way, I forgot to mention I've been having double vision for the last month' just as he's preparing to greet his next patient. Write down when your symptoms started and what makes them better or worse during a 24-hour period. .

Pamela F. Gallin, MD, a clinical professor of ophthalmology and paediatrics and the author of *How to Survive Your Doctor's Care*, suggests using a prepared script. Say, for instance, that you've been bothered by stomach pain:

I've had_____(problem) for_____(how long).
It's worse when I_____(context: eat dairy products,
bend over). The pain is_____(type: sharp, dull).
It's_____(mild, severe, intolerable) and_____
(duration: intermittent, constant). It began_____
(when: spontaneously, after taking an antibiotic
following a root canal). When I take_____
(medication: probiotic; anti-spasmodic) it makes
it____(effect: all better, partially better, doesn't
affect the pain at all).

Come clean

Understand – and remind yourself – that your relationship with your doctor is confidential. If you're doing something you're embarrassed about but want to get it off your chest – perhaps you started smoking again or you're drinking more alcohol than usual – you're in a safe place and you should open up.

Come again?

If you're uncertain about something the doctor said, don't be afraid to say so. Try repeating what you heard him say. For example, say, 'Let me make sure I've got this straight. I'm supposed to take the white pill three times a day with food and the yellow one first thing in the morning. Is that right?' And if you're still puzzled by his instructions, ask him to explain it a different way. If there are words you don't understand, ask what they mean or get the doctor to write them down so that you can look them up later.

Bring a friend

Research shows that we forget half of what we're told by the doctor when we're stressed, so bring a relative or friend with you if it will help. Be honest about what you think may be causing the problem, and don't be embarrassed. Your doctor will have seen and heard it all before.

SECOND OPINION Doctors generally expect you to trust their judgment, especially if you have a history together. But most are fine about patients seeking a second opinion when a significant course of treatment or surgery is recommended. Fully evaluate your options by gathering whatever information is needed to make an educated decision. Advice, in person, from a fully qualified professional is the only kind that counts, though. A second opinion from that very popular practitioner Dr Google doesn't.

Do better...

Eat with chopsticks

Whether lunching on sushi with the new director of the East Asian division or having dinner with your kids at Wagamama, at some point you may wish you could expertly wrangle a pair of chopsticks. The truth is, it's not that hard to get the hang of what the Chinese call 'quick little fellows'. Here's how:

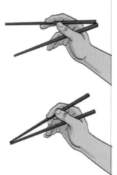

1. *Pinch the upper stick between the thumb and forefinger, resting it against the middle finger. The lower stick rests against the ring finger, with the thicker end on the crook between the thumb and forefinger.*

2. *With the two ends of the sticks even, hold the lower stick still while the upper stick moves towards it to pick up the food.*

CHOPSTICK ETIQUETTE

▸▸ Waving your chopsticks in the air during your meal is considered rude. Not to mention you might poke someone's eye out.

▸▸ Spearing your food with your chopsticks is also frowned upon. If you're having trouble, ask for a fork. And know that it is considered perfectly appropriate to eat sushi (though not sashimi) with your fingers.

▸▸ Avoid planting your chopsticks in a bowl of rice or other food. Rest them during a meal either on your plate or on the chopstick rest. If you choose the former, try to remember to place them at the bottom of your plate with the tips to the left if you're right-handed, vice versa if you're left-handed. Used chopsticks should not be placed directly on the table.

Find a **mentor**

I n secondary school, it was the teacher who nurtured your interest in chemistry and got you to enter the science fair. At university, it was the adviser who pointed you towards an internship and steered you through the application process. Robin had Batman; Luke had Yoda. Life is complicated; mentors can make it easier.

Choose wisely

'Identify someone with qualities and skills you admire or who has expertise you'd benefit from,' advises Tom McGurn, an executive with SCORE, an affiliate of the Small Business Administration in the US. 'You want someone who's objective, who praises you when you need it and can give criticism when you need it. You don't want a yes man.' When seeking a mentor at work, though, it's best not to go around your boss and ask *her* boss to coach you. In fact, according to McGurn, it's often a smart idea to find a mentor in an entirely different part of the company so you can broaden your perspective.

If you believe someone might be a good prospect, approach him with smart questions. For example, after a presentation about a new product, you might ask, 'Why did you highlight the features rather than the packaging and price?' McGurn says, 'This makes the potential mentor think, "This person listened carefully. Maybe she's worth an investment of my time".'

Don't push it

No dashing up to your target and asking, 'Will you be my mentor?' Says McGurn, 'In a lot of ways, this is like dating. It can't be rushed or forced.' As with any new relationship, connection and kinship need to develop at their own pace. 'The ideal relationship,' says McGurn, 'is one that evolves over time.' You can't hurry love – the same goes for mentoring.

Do better...

Once you've made an impression as someone who deserves some attention, suggest lunch or coffee, says Gina Rudan, an executive coach and the author of *Practical Genius: The Real Smarts You Need to Get Your Talents and Passions Working for You*. Discuss your situation and let the person know you're looking for someone to give advice and guidance and explain why you think she would be a good match for you. Follow up with an email thanking him for his time and spelling out your goals and expectations, as well as your commitment to them. This will show how serious you are.

'Interesting, smart people love a challenge,' she advises. 'If you make a strong sell for yourself, it will be hard for the mentor you're pursuing to resist.' Seed the relationship properly and make an accurate evaluation of her potential as a mentor, and she may well agree to your request on the spot.

If she asks for time to think about it or ultimately turns you down because of schedule constraints, don't take this as a rejection. You're asking a busy person to share time with you that she might not have. Better to have someone who can commit herself rather than someone who's too stretched to give you what you need. Ask her to recommend other prospects.

Set and respect boundaries

Once you've established your relationship, identify the times that are most convenient for your mentor to take your calls, answer your emails or meet with you. Stick with them. Never pump him for information or contacts; instead, take what is offered with grace and gratitude. Pressuring him for news he's not comfortable sharing or for favours he's not inclined to bestow is a surefire way to turn him off.

Finally, recognise that the connection isn't necessarily meant to last until retirement. Although plenty of such relationships evolve into lifelong friendships, just as many run their course. If you get where you were hoping to go with your mentor's help, buy him a nice dinner to say thank you and let him off the hook. Ask if you can keep in touch, though. While no longer active, the relationship is an asset you will want to maintain.

KEEP ON GIVING For help finding a mentor, the Coaching & Mentoring Network (coachingnetwork.org.uk) matches you with people, products and services. Canadian company Peer Resources Network, which does a similar job, has compiled a Mentor Hall of Fame, a list cataloguing scores of famous mentors and their equally famous mentees. Which only goes to prove that anyone can benefit from a mentor:

▸▸ Fidel Castro (President of Cuba) is political mentor to the President of Venezuela Hugo Chávez.

▸▸ Actress Uta Hagen mentored actor Jack Lemmon, who later mentored actor Kevin Spacey.

▸▸ Margaret Thatcher mentored John Major.

▸▸ Sitting Bull (Lakota Chief) mentored Gall (Hunkpapa Chief).

▸▸ Tina Turner mentored Mick Jagger.

▸▸ Muhammad Ali mentored daughter Laila Ali (female boxer) and boxer Larry 'the Easton Assassin' Holmes.

Who has helped you the most?

Do better...

Set a **table**

Forget the rulebooks and daunting images of matching finger bowls and perfectly placed fish knives. Entertaining at home should be less about which fork goes where and more about creating a warm and inviting atmosphere in which guests can relax and enjoy themselves. Yes, you want to ensure everything coordinates and is within easy reach. But more important, you want to design a table no one wants to leave.

Cover up

Think of your table as the base on which you'll build various layers – the more layers, the richer (and more formal) the result often is. You'll start with the table covering. While a plain tablecloth works perfectly well, you might want to add a sheer piece of coordinating fabric on top or a runner if your table is

long. Anyway, make sure your tablecloth is big enough to hang 15 centimetres below the table edge. Place mats are fine for a more casual affair or if you have a pretty table you want to show off.

Place the plates and glasses

Think BMW: bread plate, 'meal' plate, water glass – from left to right. The wineglass hovers to the right of the water glass.

Situate the silverware

The general rule is to lay knives and forks from the outside in, in the order they will be used. Place dessert spoons and forks across the top of the setting, the spoon above pointing left and the fork below pointing right. Folded napkins can be placed to the left of the dinner plate, beneath the silverware or on the plate itself. For a buffet, you can gather up sets of cutlery, wrap them in napkins and stack them in the centre of the table.

Create a tablescape

Of course, there's more to all this than lining up the glasses and the silverware in the right order. When you set a table, you're setting a mood. 'Things don't have to be expensive to make an impact,' says event planner Marcy Blum. 'Anytime you're at a flea market or jumble sale, look for interesting mismatched plates. You can also pick up great stuff like vases, votive candles, candleholders.' Use them to create a tablescape, a collection of small arrangements that serve as the focal point.

Traditional tablescapes include flowers. Fill a single vase with one type or, if you have a mix of vessels, try varying the blooms, placing tall-stemmed flowers in large vases, silver pitchers, footed urns and the like, and short ones in smaller containers (like bud vases or even antique teacups), while keeping the colour the same for a consistent look. Or eschew flowers altogether.

A bowl of pinecones; a large, shallow dish of river rocks; a clear cylinder vase – or three in varying sizes – half filled with coloured glass balls; or a cluster of candles set on a small antique mirror or surrounded by greenery all make nice centrepieces.

Keep guests in mind

Whatever you choose, make sure that the height of your arrangement is 30 centimetres or less to avoid blocking the view across the table and that the scent is subtle if not non-existent. No one likes to smell the heavy aroma of lilies or hyacinths while eating. If you're using place cards – and with more than six guests, it's a good idea – scribble the names on unlikely objects, like lemons or the backs of postcards.

Set up the buffet

If you're having a buffet, create a little interest by positioning serving platters at different heights, suggests Katie Brown, author of *Katie Brown Celebrates*. Stack sturdy books or boxes of varying sizes on the buffet table, drape them with a large piece of colourful fabric and top with the serving dishes. Place a menu on the table so guests will know what they're digging into.

WHAT HAPPENS AT THE TABLE Everyone knows that a great dinner party depends on more than good food. The same goes for family meals. In fact, studies have found that the effects of this ritual on kids can be profound. Researchers have shown that dinner-table conversation among families was the best predictor of children's linguistic and literary development: kids with advanced language abilities come from families who eat dinner together more often and whose conversations are filled with questions, jokes, storytelling and a lively vocabulary.

Garden
with less fuss

Is your attitude to tilling and mulching, watering and weeding like that of Victorian women to sex: why should something this boring have to take so long? Well no one needs to know that you don't have green fingers; a little planning and a little planting can deliver a big payoff. And you don't have to slog away for months – low maintenance doesn't necessarily mean low quality.

Redefine the garden

The photos of lush, complex gardens you see in magazines are the result of months and years of effort and lots and lots of money. You could have a garden like that, but you'd probably have to quit your job (and rob a bank) to do it. Instead, focus on one simple thing that gives you pleasure. Whether you live in a high-rise and have an herb pot in the windowsill or display a single fig tree in a pot on the patio of your house in the suburbs, your garden is what you say it is.

Pot it

Some plants, such as agaves and yuccas, are low maintenance with a high pizzazz factor and, like a nice piece of sculpture, make a stunning focal point in a pot. A planter filled with texturally diverse herbs – basil, dill, mint, rosemary – smells great when the plants brush against your legs as you walk by. Perhaps the best part of pot gardening is that you can easily change it seasonally, just the way you might inside your house. Say you have three big pots on your patio that you replant in spring, summer and autumn. Think of them as nine chances to show your panache with very little effort.

Make it personal

Identify shrubs, bushes, annuals or perennials that suit your personality. If you're a results-oriented person, think about growing vegetables or interesting annuals that will give you something for the table – both food and decoration. Do you see yourself as artistic? Look for plants with bright foliage or colour-saturated annuals. Is bigger always better? Think about plants with expansive flowers, like the hardy hibiscus or something that makes a giant statement, such as a banana plant. A few thriving signature plants will send more of a message than a garden full of the same old, same olds.

LAWN GAMES The idea of cultivating a perfect lawn has its roots in the Victorian aesthetic – so we have them to blame for the tens of billions we feel we have to spend on lawn care every year. But some residential renegades are saying 'No, thank you' to the traditional notion of lawns. In pockets all over the country, grass is being replaced with moss or gravel and other hardscaping that lets people get off the growing-and-mowing treadmill. Some ecological purists are allowing native plants to form a meadow where the lawn once lived. Even some professionals are giving themselves a break from the drive for perfection. If it's green and it's growing, it's grass.

Teach a child to
ride a bike

You never forget how to ride a bike, but most of us forget how hard it was to learn. That's why when adults teach children, the experience can be frustrating – for everyone. But seeing a child get his first taste of independence as he pedals off on his own is one of life's most gratifying moments, and it's worth getting it right. When a kid is up and cruising on two wheels, she might as well be leading the final stage of the Tour de France – even if she's only just started the Tour de Car Park. Here's what to keep in mind when coaxing little ones from two feet to two wheels.

Begin with the right equipment

Start with a bicycle that's the right size. A newbie should be able to sit on the seat with both feet flat on the ground. (Once your child's more proficient, you can adjust the seat so the tips of her toes touch, but for now she needs more control.) When in doubt, err on the side of a bike that's too small. If she's been using a bike with training wheels, remove them, since they ultimately make it more difficult for her to learn to balance on her own.

A good-quality, well-fitting helmet is also a must. According to the Bicycle Helmet Safety Institute, you want one that comfortably touches the head all the way around and stays in place even if you try to move it once it's strapped on. It should rest low on the head with the strap comfortably snug. When your child opens her mouth wide, she should feel the helmet pull down a little bit, and when she looks up, she should be able to see the rim of the helmet.

Long trousers and long-sleeved shirts aren't a bad idea, either, to prevent scrapes in the event of a spill. Make a steering course out of safety cones, buckets or laundry baskets, and bring along your own bike so you can demonstrate.

Find a safe spot to learn

Head to a location that has smooth, flat, open pavement and little or no traffic to distract or endanger your child. It helps if there's no one around, too, so she won't feel self-conscious. The ideal spot? A school car park at the weekend.

Emphasise the basics

The fundamentals of biking are balance, coasting, pedalling and steering.

➤ *To help a child learn to balance, have her sit on the bike seat with both feet touching the ground. Then get her to move the bike forward by pushing off with her feet.*

➤ *After she masters this, encourage her to build up momentum by lifting her feet to coast a little. Show her how she can coast with her feet very near the ground and how she can stop simply by placing her feet down.*

➤ *Once she's a confident coaster, it's time to pedal. Have her stand over the bike with one foot on the ground and one on a pedal, which should be positioned at about 2 o'clock. Before beginning, remind her how to put her feet down in order to stop the bike or regain balance. Instruct her to push down on the pedal with the first foot while placing the other foot on the other pedal just as she begins to move forwards. You can place your hand on the back of the seat to reassure and steady her as soon as she is in motion, and then let go. Remind her to keep her feet moving. No doubt there will be more than a few stops and starts and maybe even a wipeout or two. But eventually she will manage to ride a fair stretch without stopping or falling. When she does, encourage her to slow down and then drop her feet to the ground to stop.*

▸▸ *After several successful straight runs, introduce steering. Start by making her ride in large circles that give her the feel of controlling the bike's direction. Then set up a few of the cones or other markers (about 5m apart) and get her to practise weaving in and out of them. Eventually, she'll master her turns, her speed and her stops.*

▸▸ *When she's really comfortable riding and steering, talk about using the brakes to stop the bike. Whether that means pedal brakes or hand brakes, emphasise slowing down before braking gently. The abrupt use of brakes causes more spills than any other aspects of riding, so hammer home the 'gently' part.*

Now practise – a lot

After a fair number of dry runs, it's time to move to the big stage. Find a bike path or a little-travelled street in a residential area where you can demonstrate how to share the road with cars – riding with, not against, the traffic. Cycle along with the child to check that she's using proper safety techniques and feels comfortable pedalling in traffic.

BIKE ABILITY If you feel your child needs lessons, there are many cycling schemes out there to help kids learn to ride. Developed by more than 20 organisations, including the Royal Society for Prevention against Accidents, Bikeability (dft.gov.uk/bikeability) has been set up to give kids – and adults – the skills and confidence to ride on the roads. A child will typically start Bikeability lessons once they have learnt to ride a bike, with 10–11 year olds progressing to Level 2, and then Level 3 at secondary school. Certificates and shiny badges are awarded to children who complete each level.

Tell a great
bedtime story

You raise a reader by reading to her – and who doesn't cherish memories of being lulled to sleep by the words of *Snow White* or *Peter Pan*? Even better, though, are stories Mum, Dad and Grandpa seem to create from thin air, as a fairy godmother does a pair of glass slippers. Knowing how to dream up a story that keeps them on the edge of their bunk beds will make you the Great Oz, Harry Potter and Hannah Montana all rolled into one. Here's how to create a memorable night-time fable.

Start it off right
The first few words are what grab little listeners' often wandering attention. There are a million ways to go, but if you're stuck, the classic fairy tale approach usually does the trick: 'Once upon a time...' 'A long, long time ago...' 'In a far-off land, there was once...'

Create a hero
Kids like familiar characters and tales that build on what's gone before. Try telling a different story each night about Spike, the family dog; his imaginary girlfriend Petunia; and their many misadventures. Or get your child to be the protagonist. Be sure to establish some character traits that can help set up a familiar theme: 'Billy always liked to be the first one in line.' Or 'Sean was always grumpy in the morning until he'd had his bowl of ice cream.'

Now what happens?
The action should begin with a single event, such as a package arriving in the post. Then weave your child's favourite things, activities and colours into your story. 'Sally opened the door,

and there was a purple alien named Violet on the front step!'
Somewhere in the middle, there needs to be a surprise, problem
or crisis. 'Sally got a letter saying that MI5 were coming to
take Violet away!' The rest of the story is then about how that
problem gets solved.

Make it crackle

Classic story lines involve journeys, quests, mysteries or
contests – and give you plenty of opportunities to add plot
twists and details. Dazzle them with vivid imagery, detailed
descriptions and the most evocative words you can think of.
Don't just use verbs; use smash-bam-pow action verbs. Don't
just give the heroine dark hair; give her hair the colour of
midnight on a moonless night.

Wrap it up

Before you reach the end, begin to wind the story down, then
wrap it up with a happy resolution. Speak more slowly and
quietly as you near the conclusion so your child can leave
the excitement behind and smoothly drift off into dreamland.
Visions of sugarplums are strictly optional.

ADVICE FROM A MASTER Best-selling author Lemony Snicket
shares his tips for telling a great bedtime story:

▸▸ 'Ask your child what the title should be. This stalls for time
and spreads the blame if the story's no good.'

▸▸ 'Name the villains after people who wronged you at school.'

▸▸ 'When you get stuck, remember Raymond Chandler's
advice: "When in doubt, have two guys come through
the door with guns." The bedtime equivalent is a clumsy
talking animal holding a tray of cream pies.'

Mix a perfect **martini**

'I am prepared to believe that a dry martini slightly impairs the palate,' novelist Alec Waugh once wrote, 'but think what it does for the soul.' Whether it was invented by a bartender in Martinez, California, during the gold rush; named for a British rifle called the Martini-Henry because of its kick; or first concocted for John D. Rockefeller at the Knickerbocker Hotel in 1911, by the time James Bond was ordering one on-screen (to oft-quoted specifications), the martini had become the liquid epitome of cool. Here's how to mix up a perfect one:

1. *The ideal martini is ice cold. Start by chilling the following in the freezer for at least an hour:*

   ▸▸ Gin (a premium brand)

   ▸▸ Dry vermouth (we like Noilly Pratt)

   ▸▸ Martini glasses

   ▸▸ A cocktail shaker or a glass jug (you'll need the latter if you, like Bond, prefer your drink stirred, not shaken)

2. *Have the following ready, too:*

   ▸▸ A strainer

   ▸▸ A stirrer (if you're using a jug)

   ▸▸ Cracked ice cubes, preferably made from bottled water

   ▸▸ Cocktail olives and sticks

   ▸▸ A cutting board, a lemon and a sharp paring knife (if a twist is your garnish)

3. *Once your liquor and glassware are chilled, combine 5 parts gin to 1 part vermouth in either a cocktail shaker or jug almost filled with ice (to make an extra-dry martini, reduce the vermouth to just a splash). If you are using a jug, stir the mixture briskly about 20 times. If you are using a shaker, cover it and shake vigorously several times.*

4. *Strain the mixture into the ice-cold glasses, taking care not to let any of the ice into the glass. Pierce two olives with a cocktail stick and place one stick in each glass. Or, if you prefer a twist, pare a 5cm strip of lemon peel for each glass, and wring one over each glass to release the lemon oil; then set the peel on the edge of the glass.*

5. *Serve the drink by the stem of the glass to keep it chilled. Then toast your good fortune as you enjoy one of life's great potable pleasures.*

MARTINI MECCA Nick Strangeway, one of the world's most celebrated bartenders, insists that Dukes Hotel in London is the place to go to experience the ultimate – truly the perfect – martini. At Dukes, the bartender pushes a hundred-year-old trolley from table to table, mixing the cocktails for each patron in a wonderful display of old-school elegance. Most interesting to martini aficionados, perhaps, is the fact that the Dukes martini is neither shaken nor stirred; instead, the ingredients are poured directly into the chilled glass – first the vermouth, then the gin and finally the twist.

Complain effectively

Complaining has a bad reputation. 'People either think it's pointless or that it puts them in a bad light,' says Ellen Phillips, the author of *Shocked, Appalled and Dismayed!: How to Write Letters of Complaint That Get Results*. 'We want to be liked, and we think complaining makes us seem like we're whining.' But Phillips has no qualms about it. 'I see it as standing up for myself,' she says. 'I work hard for what I earn, and if I pay good money for something and I don't get the quality I paid for, I have a right and an obligation to complain.' If you have a grievance, then air it – but don't start World War III straight away. Calm down first; then follow these steps.

Get your ducks in a row

Exhaust all the traditional channels to resolve your issue. Call customer services and follow up in writing. Be sure to note names and titles of everyone you speak with, as well as the date and time of each call. Have your receipt and notes about your previous attempts to get satisfaction. Look online for complaints about the product or company that are similar to yours.

Go right to the top

If after several attempts you're still unhappy, don't waste your time further with customer service. Instead, write a letter to the managing director of the company or the CEO – the person with the authority to right the wrong.

Start with an attention getter

You want to make sure your letter stands out, says Phillips, who suggests something like 'I am shocked by the reprehensible way I've been treated by your company.' Then tell your story in bullet points so that each piece of your account is clear. If, for example, the problem is with a washing machine, indicate where and when you purchased it and what the issue is: did it arrive broken? Did it start malfunctioning the third time you used it? Then explain what you did to try to fix the problem. Once you've given the background information, be clear about what you want – a refund? a replacement? an apology? – and when you expect to hear back. Phillips warns, 'If you're not specific about what you want, you're not going to get anything.'

Make it clear that you mean business

Do not make threats about legal action. If you remain calm and measured, you are more likely to be taken seriously. If you rant and rave about lawyers and legal action striaght away, you may get treated like a crackpot. If you are still unhappy after you have complained to the retailer or service provider, check the Office of Fair Trading website (Oft.gov.uk) and contact the Citizens Advice Bureau, Adviceguide.org.uk, to find out what you can do next and the relevant consumer organisation to contact. Let the company know that you intend to take further action and don't underestimate the power of a complaint on Facebook, Twitter or other social media and consumer complaint websites. Bad publicity works wonders and sometimes gets fast results.

Say thank you

If your complaint campaign ultimately succeeds, be sure to thank the person or people who were able to help straighten things out. If someone was truly heroic, be sure to tell his or her boss.

Look at the big picture

'People often say, 'I'm not going to try to resolve this issue, because no one's going to listen to me,' ' says Phillips. 'And if they do try and get no response, they never make another attempt. It would be nice to think that our very first letter is going to be answered – and answered in the way that we'd like. But if it isn't, we have to keep trying. Otherwise, we're giving the company or the store permission to keep on doing what it's doing.'

Knot a **tie**

In a world of dress-down Mondays-through-Fridays, a tie says, 'I'm a serious grown-up you can count on.' It makes a great first impression and is easy to do if you follow these steps:

1. *Standing in front of a mirror, wrap the tie around your neck, with the wide end of the tie on the right side and the narrow end on the left. The wide end should extend about 30cm below the narrow end.*

2. *Cross the wide end of the tie over the top of the narrow end.*

3. *Loop the wide end around the back of the narrow end of the tie.*

Do better...

4. *Continue by bringing the wide end back over in front of the narrow end again.*

5. *Pull the wide end behind the narrow end again, then up through the Y shape formed at your neckline.*

6. *Still holding the wide end, pull it down through the loop you just created.*

7. *Holding the narrow end with one hand, slide the knot up to tighten the tie, finishing with the wide end slightly longer than the narrow end, hitting at or just below the navel. Finally, feed the narrow end through the brand label on the back of the wide end.*

And what about the bow tie?

When the occasion calls for something fancy, go authentic.
Ditch the clip-on and follow this guide to tying the real deal:

1. *Standing in front of a mirror, place the tie around your neck, with end A about 5cm longer than end B.*

2. *Cross end A over end B.*

3. *Pull end A up through the loop at the neck.*

4. *Double end B over itself to form the first loop of the bow tie.*

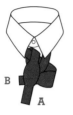

5. *Loop end A over the loop you just created.*

6. *Here's the tricky part: double end A over itself, and tuck it into the loop at the back of the bow tie.*

7. *Tighten by tugging at the ends, making sure they are even.*

ON THE WAY OUT? A poll of 2,000 British workers by online bank First Direct found that only one in 10 employees wears a suit every day and only 18 per cent regularly wear a tie. Cary Cooper, professor of organisational psychology at Lancaster University management school, agrees that the world has moved on and the tie has had its day. 'What is the point of a tie? It's the weirdest thing. If someone from Mars went into an office the first question they'd ask is "What's that thing round your neck?"'

Make a **toast**

It's going to happen. One day you will have to stand up, glass in hand, and clear your throat or knock some cutlery against the side of a champagne flute. Maybe you'll have had time to memorise every syllable, but more likely, you won't have a clue it's going to happen until someone hands you a mic. Either way, follow these steps and you'll acquit yourself nicely.

Find a friendly face
God willing, this will be the person or couple you're toasting. Raise your glass, and give them a smile. This little gift is from you to them. If there happen to be 250 other people in the room eavesdropping, so be it.

Know the room
People wince when you get things wrong, and when you get something wrong in a toast, they really wince. Remember, the toast at the bachelor party isn't the same as the toast at the wedding – in tone, language or content – and the audience isn't the same, either. If you're toasting at the latter, don't mention ex-girlfriends, recount insane drunken nights out or forget to mention the bride.

Introduce yourself
Ever been to an event where someone gets up and just starts talking? 'Can you believe Linda and Larry have been married for half a century? I remember when they first joined our bowling team... blah, blah, blah.' No one cares whatever what's-her-name is saying. They're all too busy asking each other, 'Who the heck is she?' So before you utter your first word, introduce yourself and tell everyone how you know the person you're toasting.

Be funny

We don't mean a-chimp-and-a-donkey-walk-into-a-bar funny. Chances are, if you've been asked to make a toast, you know the toastees fairly well. Make it relevant-to-the-occasion amusing. Pick a short anecdote that illustrates something about their personalities. For example: 'I knew Stacey and Darren were made for each other when Stacey told me they both always dreamed of a road trip to Dollywood.'

Then leave them misty-eyed

Funny is fine, but it's also important to lend some gravitas to the occasion. The best way is to speak from the heart and be specific. A few words packed with genuine emotion go a long way. A retirement dinner? Talk about what a difference the honoree has made in the lives of those in the room. A wedding? Choose one detail to end on. 'I'm sure your honeymoon in Dollywood will be great, but here's to the wild and wonderful roller-coaster ride of marriage that begins right now.'

MEMORABLE MOVIE TOASTS

▶▶ 'A toast to my big brother George. The richest man in town.'
– Todd Karns in *It's a Wonderful Life*

▶▶ 'Here's looking at you, kid.'
– Humphrey Bogart in *Casablanca*

▶▶ 'Never lie, steal, cheat or drink. But if you must lie, lie in the arms of the one you love. If you must steal, steal away from bad company. If you must cheat, cheat death. And if you must drink, drink in the moments that take your breath away.'
– Will Smith in *Hitch*

Cure the
hiccups

Hiccups are one of life's more annoying predicaments, and they start when the vagus nerve (which runs from your brain to your abdomen) is irritated. Your diaphragm contracts involuntarily, and that sets off a sudden closure of your vocal cords, which produces that telltale 'hic' sound. So how do you stop them?

Calm your vagus nerve

The following tactics may help overwhelm the impulse pattern and stop your hiccups:

➤ *Suck a wedge of lemon soaked in Angostura bitters. This treatment is said to work almost instantly. Before you go searching the pantry for the bitters, you might try chewing on just the lemon. Several sources say the sour sensation alone will be enough to do the trick.*

➤ *Hold your hands over your ears. Branches of the vagus nerve reach into the auditory system, so stimulating the nerve endings there can throw off the hiccup pattern.*

➤ *Create an interruption.*

➤ *If your hiccups last hours or even days, try acupuncture. In one study done at the National Institutes of Health, 13 out of 16 patients with persistent hiccups were cured in one to three sessions over a one- to seven-day period. The other three experienced significant improvement.*

These tricks are designed to interrupt the spasms that are causing your hiccups:

Do better...

- *Breathe into a paper bag. This increases the amount of carbon dioxide in your system and may help stop the spasms.*

- *Guzzle a glass of warm water without stopping. Some say the warmth soothes and relaxes the diaphragm.*

- *Gargle with iced water. The cold reportedly shocks hiccups into submission.*

- *Eat a teaspoon of sugar, a tablespoon of peanut butter or a spoonful of honey. Swallowing the sticky sweetness is supposed to change the rhythm of your breathing.*

Go acid-free

Hiccups are sometimes set off by acid in the oesophagus. Lay off the spicy food and the alcohol. If that doesn't work, try an antacid. And if your hiccups continue or recur often, see your doctor. They could be a symptom of acid reflux.

Do you have a personal cure?

Do maths
in your head

So many of us rely on a smartphone these days to tally our tips or add up bills, our maths skills are eroding faster than a polar ice cap. But what happens when you can't put your hands on your mobile – or even a pad and pencil – to come up with answers? Simple. Use your head (and a few easy tricks).

Working out a tip

If 10 per cent is the standard tip in your area, simply move the decimal point one place to the left to divide the bill total by 10. For a bill of £92.90, the tip would be £9.29. If your server was especially good, you may want to round this up.

Calculating compound interest

This is a trick that can help you determine how much that new car/house/dress is *really* going to cost you. Say you want to borrow £10,000 to do some home improvements and you're considering a 5-year loan at 8 per cent interest. Here's a quick way to figure it out:

Since you're making regular inroads into the capital as you go, calculate the interest on about half the amount of the loan, or £5,000, which we'll call the average value of the debt. Multiply that £5,000 by the interest rate (0.08) and you get £400, which is the average annual interest on your average debt. To account for compound interest (the interest on the interest), add another 10 per cent of your average interest, or £40 to your average interest, for a total of £440. Multiply that by the number of years of the loan (5) and you get £2,200, which is the rough cost of the loan.

Dividing by 5

At a nature reserve, a ranger notes the reserve's size as being 840 square kilometres and reveals, among other things, that there's an average of 1 coppiced sessile oak to every 5 square kilometres. How many trees are we talking about here? To quickly divide a large number by 5, think 2. In this case, multiply the large number by 2 in your head (840 x 2 = 1,680), then simply knock off the zero. Your quick and easy answer for the number of these ancient trees: 168.

Multiplying by 9

If you've long since forgotten your multiplication tables, this good old-fashioned finger maths trick can help you multiply any number from 1 to 10 by 9:

▸▸ *Spread your two hands out in front of you.*

▸▸ *To multiply 9 x 4, fold down the 4th finger from your left little finger (this would be your index finger). If you were to multiply by 7, you would fold down the 7th finger from the left little finger, and so on.*

▸▸ *Now look at your hands. You have 3 fingers to the left of your bent index finger and 6 to the right – your answer is 36.*

(Or you could learn your multiplication tables in the lower juniors like everyone else.)

The amazing 11 rule

The 10 rule is easy (to multiply by 10, just add a zero at the end of the number). The 11 rule is much cooler. To multiply a two-digit number by 11, using the number 43 as an example:

▸▸ *Separate the two digits in your head (4__3)*

▸▸ *Add the two digits together (4 + 3 = 7)*

▸▸ *Put the sum of 7 in the hole between the 4 and 3 and there's your answer – 11 x 43 = 473*

▸▸ *If the sum of the two digits is greater than 9, you put only the 'ones' digit in the hole between the numbers, then add the 'tens' digit to the left-hand number. So to multiply 11 by the number 49, for example: 4__9; 4 + 9 = 13; put the 3 in the hole (439) and add the 1 from the 13 to the 4 to get a final result of 539; 11 x 49 = 539.*

Converting kilometres to miles

Approximate this way: take the first digit of the kilometre figure and multiply it by 6. For example, take the 8 in 84 kilometre and multiply it by 6. The answer, 48, is the rough equivalent in miles. (The exact equivalent is 52.19, but 48 is close enough for most purposes.)

CALCULATE YOUR SUCCESS According to the Rand Corporation, a Washington, D.C., think tank, couples in the US who can answer the following three simple maths questions tend to be more than eight times wealthier than those who can't.

1. *If the chance of getting a disease is 10 per cent, how many people out of 1,000 would be expected to get the disease?*

2. *If five people all have the winning numbers in the lottery and the prize is $2 million, how much will each of them get?*

3. *If you have $200 in a savings account and the account earns 10 per cent interest a year, how much would you have in the account at the end of two years?*

Answers: 1) 100; 2) $400,000; 3) $242

Iron a shirt

Nothing says 'I'm your man (or woman)!' like a crisply ironed shirt. After shined shoes, a professionally ironed shirt is the No. 1 signal to your boss, your client or that certain someone you're trying to impress that you are dressed for success. Here's how to do it:

1. *Fill your iron with cool water. Set the iron to the temperature appropriate for the fabric. When the iron is hot, enable the steam feature.*

2. *Start with the collar. Spread it face down on the ironing board. Press the iron from the tip to the middle, then repeat on the other side. (Iron the inside of the collar last, after Step 5.)*

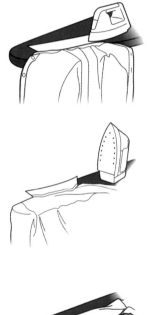

3. *Next comes the back yoke. Spread the shirt over the tapered end of the ironing board so that the yoke is flat and the tip of the ironing board is tucked slightly into one sleeve. Iron half the yoke, and then adjust the shirt so the tip of the board is tucked into the other sleeve. Iron the other half.*

4. *Now the sleeves. Unbutton the cuffs and flatten one on the board. Press. Then take that sleeve and lie it flat on the*

ironing board with the seam closest to you. Iron the sleeve from the shoulder to the cuff, being careful to end up with a single crease. Repeat with the other sleeve.

5. *To iron the body of the shirt, position one half of the front of the shirt at the tapered end of the ironing board so that the tip of the board is tucked slightly into the top of the sleeve. Start at the top, and – being careful not to make creases near the collar – work your way down to the bottom of the shirt. Adjust the shirt on the ironing board to iron one half of the back, working from the yoke to the bottom hem, and then repeat with the other half. Finish with the other half of the front of the shirt.*

❝For a crisp look to your shirt, spray the entire shirt *lightly* with spray starch, then roll it up for 60 seconds to let the starch set into the fabric before ironing.❞

– Barbara Zagnoni, ironing expert and Rowenta's 'Queen of Steam'

6. *Finally, press the inside of the collar, from the points to the middle. Now hang this beautiful item on a hanger and button the top two buttons to help the shirt retain its shape.*

IRON-CLAD TRICKS

▶▶ Hang shirts on a coathanger straight from the dryer to minimise deep wrinkles.

▶▶ Keep your iron and ironing board clean.

▶▶ Keep the iron moving to avoid scorching the fabric.

▶▶ Use the tip of the iron to work around buttons, cuffs and collar.

▶▶ Never iron a shirt that isn't clean; this will set stains.

Master the art of
self-defence

Whether you're trying to avoid an altercation with a stranger or trying to keep your cool when a frenemy trashes your idea at work, it helps to know how to take charge calmly, authoritatively and without raising either your voice or your fist. These tips will help you smooth things over and (quietly) come out on top.

The 'Don't even think about it' look

Conveying confidence can defuse a difficult situation before it starts, and one of the best ways to do that is through eye contact. If you find yourself ready to argue with someone about who's first in line at the take-away, stand tall, lock eyes and hold the other person's gaze until he grows uncomfortable and turns away. Done right, it'll ensure he knows who's boss without saying a word. This works particularly well with youngsters and dogs.

The 'You're right – I'm a moron' manoeuvre

Sometimes a hint of levity – particularly of the self-deprecating variety – can ease a tense situation. When a co-worker starts undercutting you in a meeting, adopt friendly, open, non-aggressive body language and say something like 'Hey, Dan, to be honest, I sometimes talk too much. But in this case, I think I might be onto something.' Then simply confront the accusation in a lighthearted manner and defend your own position. Be careful to avoid giving the impression you're making fun of your adversary, though, or you might end up fanning the flames.

The 'Kill them with kindness' trick

As Mark Twain once said, 'Kindness is a language which the deaf can hear and the blind can see.' That's why this trick works like a charm. She makes a dig about your outfit? You compliment hers. He makes a rude remark about your cooking? You offer a generous second helping. She makes a crack about your kid? You make a friendly fuss over hers. This is the foolproof smiley-face umbrella you use when someone's trying to rain on your parade. And unless the meanie is a sociopath, he or she will feel like an idiot for having been so nasty to someone so nice and have no reason to keep goading you, since you obviously won't play.

The 'Melon eye-gouge' move

OK, everyone needs a fallback strategy in case the Look, the Manoeuvre or the Trick goes hopelessly awry and triggers an actual physical altercation. If you're ever in a truly life-threatening situation, here's what to do: you know how you pick up a melon in a supermarket and squeeze it to check for ripeness? That's just what you'd do when sticking your thumbs in a bad guy's eyes before running for safety. Practise this move in the fruit aisle every week and you'll be ready for anything.

Have you ever stood up to someone?

Get a good night's sleep

Poets and authors can't rhapsodise enough about sleep. It's the 'balm of hurt minds' and 'nature's soft nurse' (Shakespeare), a 'gentle thing' (Coleridge), something that 'covers a man all over, thoughts and all, like a cloak' (Cervantes). But where are the wise words about how to catch the ZZZs that are essential for good health? Try these.

Eat, drink and treat your way to sleep

Poultry, eggs, nuts and other foods rich in tryptophan – a chemical used in the synthesis of sleep-inducing hormones serotonin and melatonin – can help. Avoid chocolate, which contains caffeine, and sugary bedtime snacks. When choosing beverages, go with warm milk or camomile or peppermint tea, which all promote relaxation and shut-eye, instead of caffeinated drinks or alcohol – classic sleep busters. Even moderate caffeine consumption during the day can be a deterrent to sleep at night (it remains in your system for hours). And while a glass of wine may help you feel tired at first, it ultimately interrupts your sleep. Sometimes a magnesium supplement can aid the regularly sleep-deprived. Treating heartburn (and allergies) is also key.

Develop a bedtime ritual

By following the same nightly routine – washing your face, brushing your teeth, spending a few minutes meditating – you're sending your body a simple but powerful signal that now is the time to start winding down. A bath, a good book and some soft music may also help. Head for bed around the same hour every night. And when you get up in the morning, sit, close your eyes and start your day with peace and gratitude. Setting a serene tone for the day can reduce the stress hormones that keep you awake at night.

Do better...

Declutter your brain

Every time you start thinking about bills unpaid, work not done or children gone astray, shift your mind to something less stimulating. Deep breathing is a great stress reducer and can distract you from your worries. Lie on your back and inhale as deeply as you can through your nose, counting slowly to 10 in your head. Then slowly and gently exhale for the same count through your mouth. Repeat several times.

Keep a worry book

Put a notebook and pen beside your bed. When you wake up and start worrying, jot down everything that's bothering you, along with any strategies you've thought of that will solve the problems to which they're related. Then close the book, put it on your bedside table, turn out the light and go back to sleep. Your worries will be waiting for you in the morning.

Think like Goldilocks

Choose a comfortable mattress (not too hard, not too soft) that properly supports your body. Test several for comfort and firmness before you buy. Even better, find a mattress store

that offers a 30-day trial period. Rotate your mattress routinely so that it wears evenly and retains its firmness for as long as possible. And when you suspect your mattress is 'going', do not put off getting a replacement, or your body and your sleep will suffer. If the person on each side of the bed has his or her own sheet and blanket, there's less tugging and more sleep.

Create a sleep zone

Take an hour before your bedtime to wind down and make a conscious transition from busy, wide-awake person to peaceful, ready-to-sleep person. Quit the chores, quit the homework with the kids, quit getting involved with Facebook chats. Rid the bedroom of electronics like laptops, BlackBerrys, and even your television. Spritz a bit of lavender water around your pillow; studies show that the scent can ease insomnia. Keep the lights low and the temperature three or four degrees cooler than your normal setting; lower temperatures are a signal to your body to chill out.

DAYTIME CURES FOR NIGHT-TIME TROUBLES Exercise is good for just about everything. It reduces stress, clears the mind and, it turns out, helps you sleep as well as most medications. As little as 20 minutes of regular exercise that takes place at least two hours before bedtime can reduce the time it takes to get to sleep by 12 minutes and increase the overall amount of sleep by 42 minutes. And if you're burning the candle at both ends and just can't catch up on your sleep, go ahead and take a nap during the day. A nap between the hours of 1 and 4 P.M. will reduce your sleep debt and invigorate your day without affecting your night sleep. Even a 20-minute nap during your lunch hour can make a difference in your job performance and reduce the stress that might otherwise keep you up at night.

Do better...

Leave a **legacy**

'**W**e cannot change the cards we are dealt, just how we play the hand.' This wisdom helped the late professor Randy Pausch's talk, 'The Last Lecture' become a viral video on YouTube and a best-selling book. At the time, the computer scientist was fighting pancreatic cancer, which gave his words extra punch. Pausch stressed that we must seize every moment, which includes helping others achieve their dreams. The words were his parting gift to family and students. Below are some ideas to get you started on creating your own legacy.

Create an ethical will – now

Following Pausch's example of creating a meaningful record of experiences and values now – no matter how young you are – is a good idea, suggests author Jo Kline Cebuhar, who calls this type of written reckoning an ethical will.

An ethical will is not a legal document, stresses Cebuhar. 'It's going to be shared with the people you choose to share it with, when you want to share it,' she says. In her book, *So Grows the Tree: Creating an Ethical Will,* Cebuhar says that leaving behind life lessons, wishes and dreams may even last longer with loved ones than a financial reward.

Cebuhar got hooked on the idea about a decade ago, when she discovered a letter from an uncle who had died 25 years earlier. In the note, he emphasised the importance of keeping an open mind. 'It was priceless to find such a poignant record of his values in his own words,' says Cebuhar, who is also an attorney. 'I realised that there's a common thread of morals and beliefs in my family, and the same can be said for every family.'

Make use of special occasions

An ethical-spiritual will is a document designed to pass ethical values from one generation to the next. While it may have more urgency for baby boomers, it need not be only a late-in-life exercise to pass down to loved ones. 'I've seen people use this technique to write a letter describing their hopes for the future when a child is born. Or to a young person when they graduate or get married,' says Cebuhar. A job change, divorce or other life adjustment presents a great time to put your beliefs and feelings on paper. 'You can also make it a serial exercise – write a note on your kid's class picture every year, or add something personal to holiday letters before you stick them in the folder.' But most important? 'Just write something,' says Cebuhar. 'You'll be surprised where your hand will take you.'

WILL YOUR CREATIVE SIDE

- ▸▸ Start with a quotation from someone else that expresses your worldview, and explain why. If you get blocked, simply write at the top, 'Other people found the words I can't find. This is how I look at life.'

- ▸▸ Pick a moment in your personal history – when we landed on the moon, the first time you fell in love – and write about how it affected you.

- ▸▸ Think of three words that capture your essence. Elaborate on them with stories from your life and your hopes for the future.

- ▸▸ Embellish a family tree or photo album with anecdotes. Describe what each person taught you or a vivid memory of him or her.

- ▸▸ Find a song or song lyrics that express a sentiment you want to share.

- ▸▸ Think beyond pen and paper. Record your own videos, post inspiring thoughts on your Facebook page or find your own way to express yourself.

Do better...

Run a **meeting**

Office meetings can be a chance to get things done – in between the clueless musings and pompous pontificating of work colleagues. So when it's your turn to take charge, run yours the way Lewis Hamilton approaches Formula 1: fast, focused and sure of your goals. If you can lead a successful meeting, not only will your colleagues thank you but your boss will take notice, too. Here are a few tricks from Al Pittampalli, author of *Read This Before Our Meeting*.

Choose the participants

Too many people just clog up the works. Unless someone brings something to the table – information needed to make a decision, the authority to approve it, the responsibility to carry it through – leave him off the guest list.

Distribute an agenda

A meeting organised around brainstorming or catching up is likely to meander. Without a specific topic, people don't know how to get ready, and that's when things devolve into discussions of Ann Widdecombe and *Strictly Come Dancing*. Instead, map out a very specific list of what you want to cover, and set a time limit for each item on the agenda. Give people homework assignments: 'Come with at least two possible solutions to the problem we will be discussing.'

Find the right place

Conduct your meeting around a circular conference table. Rectangular tables invite the apple polishers to dive towards positions near the head. Chairs in rows facing the front of the room squash participation because people tend to disengage when they can't see one another.

Start with a bang

The beginning of the meeting sets the tone. Don't waste time thanking people for coming or talking pleasantries. If you did a good job preparing people, they should have arrived ready to play.

Pilot the vessel

Stay focused on your objective. What decision has to be made by the end of the meeting? Is what's being discussed getting you closer or further away? Offer prompts, ask questions, solicit input from the appropriate person at the appropriate time. It's your job to politely cut people off when necessary and redirect the conversation when it veers off track. And be sure to enforce good behaviour. No interrupting, no incivility, no mobile phones, no BlackBerrys.

Focus on action

A meeting isn't successful unless it ends with a concrete plan of action, with people assigned to take on each piece of it. Every step should have an owner and a due date. Make sure you send out the plan to every participant immediately after the meeting, and follow up to hold each accountable for his role.

OR TRY THIS Most meetings are called to share information or to reach a resolution. Pittampalli prefers a more efficient version that he calls the Modern Meeting. How does it work? 'Make your decision first,' he says. 'Then call a meeting with only the people the decision impacts, to get buy-in or feedback that will refine your approach to executing the decision. It makes things move much faster.'

How do you motivate your colleagues?

Acknowledgments

PROJECT STAFF
***Reader's Digest* Magazine**
  Vice-President, Global Editor-in-Chief Peggy Northrop
  Executive Editor Tom Prince
  Managing Editor Ann Powell
  Senior Editor Beth Dreher
  Assistant Managing Editor Paul Silverman
  Copy Editor Janice K. Bryant
  Editorial Assistant Elizabeth Kelly

Contributing Writers Fred Dubose, Sean Elder, Juliann Garey, Joanne Kaufman, Joe Kita, Gwen Moran, Hilary Sterne, Marcia Layton Turner, Jeff Wuorio

Project Editor Karen Watts
Copy Editor Barbara Booth
Consulting Art Director Elizabeth Tunnicliffe
Interior Design Vertigo Design LLC
Cover Design Robert Newman
Illustrations © Paul Boston/Meiklejohn.co.uk
                except for the following:
                Pages 50–51 © Graham White, NB Illustration
                Pages 103 and 131: © John Ley, A3 Design
                Pages 150–153, and 162: © Melanie Powell

TRADE PUBLISHING
President and Publisher Harold Clarke
Associate Publisher Rosanne McManus
Executive Editor Dolores York
Senior Art Director George McKeon

FOR VIVAT DIRECT:
Project Editor Penny Craig
Art Editor Conorde Clarke

Also Available from Reader's Digest

ISBN 978-1-78020-136-8